Made for Love

'The African marries and then falls in love.'
A traditional African saying

'I met her, and it was love at first sight.'
A Western saying

Marriage in Africa is radically different from
marriage in the West. From the moment that a
father starts to look for a wife for his son, to the
first formal meetings of the two families, and to
the way the marriage is lived in everyday life, the
relationship is marked out as African through and
through.

African culture brings many rich things into a
marriage. But it can also bring its own crop of
problems. In *Made for Love*, Ken Okeke explores
the richness and the difficulties. He examines the
role of the wider family, the increasing invasion of
Western liberal practices, the treatment of wives in
polygamy and divorce, and the value and promise
of being married for life. The book shows how a
Christian understanding of marriage can
overcome problems and turn marriage into the
positive, loving relationship it is meant to be.

The Rev. Ken Okeke was born in Nigeria and is
chaplain to Nigerians living in the United
Kingdom. He was formerly principal of the
Anglican College of Commerce at Offa in Nigeria.
He is married with three children and has long
worked among young people and young adults.

MADE FOR LOVE

MARRIAGE AS IT WAS MEANT TO BE...

KEN OKEKE

A LION
INTERNATIONAL PAPERBACK
Tring · Belleville · Sydney

Copyright © 1986 Ken S. E. Okeke

Published by
Lion Publishing plc
Icknield Way, Tring, Herts, England
ISBN 0 85648 932 8
Lion Publishing Corporation
10885 Textile Road, Belleville, Michigan 48111, USA
ISBN 0 85648 932 8
Albatross Books Pty Ltd
PO Box 320, Sutherland, NSW 2232, Australia
ISBN 0 86760 805 6

First edition 1986

Printed by
Cox & Wyman Ltd, Reading

To my parents, from whom I saw what a Christian family should be

Contents

Introduction

When people say 'I love you', one often wonders whether they really mean what they say. And when people stand before a minister in church or a marriage registrar and make marriage vows, one again wonders whether they really understand the full implications.

From experiences and observation, it can be easily seen that many people fall short of their vows. This is either because they simply cannot cope or because they never fully understood what they were going into. As a result, marriage has become something that many people are afraid of.

This book is intended to be an encouragement to anyone already married or thinking of getting married. Examining love and marriage from the African Christian perspective not only makes for an interesting study but also gives a demonstration of the possibilities in marriage. Marriage is a universal thing and in its universality God has given a recipe for happiness and fulfilment. How closely we follow this recipe determines how happy our marriage will be.

African Christians live within a society very rich in culture and they can afford to pattern their marriages along culturally accepted lines. But is that what makes their marriages happy? This book is intended to show that happiness only comes when God's standard is applied in marriage. God's standards, as presented in the Bible, transcend culture and therefore can be applied to any culture and race.

This book does not give all the answers and does not deal in superlatives. It only tries to show that ordinary human beings, trusting in God's help, can make the best out of what frightens many people today.

In writing this book I have drawn from the experiences of many different people and have used illustrations from what I have observed. The events talked about are all true, but the names and places have been altered for obvious reasons. Any resemblance therefore is pure coincidence and is not designed to be so.

I have also been inspired by Ngozi, my wife, partner and mate, who not only corrected but typed the first draft. Looking back on our twelve years of marriage it all looks as if we met yesterday.

It is my earnest desire that this book will inspire and encourage whoever reads it and also will help us all to see that marriage *can* be bliss.

Ken S. E. Okeke

1

What is Christian Marriage?

Peter and Esther might have been mistaken for newly-weds, but for two obvious facts: first their age, and second, their first son was twenty years old. Their actions and attitudes, the expression of love and concern for each other in so many little ways, was amazing to see.

By 1953, Peter and Esther had been married for twenty-five years. First-generation African Christians with five children, their family life was impressive. Peter played the role of the head of the house, yet Esther had a say in every matter. There was always laughter in the home and that made them all feel good. There was harmony, there was fun, and all was peaceful.

Some people regarded their set-up as not typically African and therefore not 'normal'. Others simply wondered what kept them the way they were. The children were well-behaved (though not little angels) both in and out of the house and you could always pick them out among other children in school. Their secret was not difficult to discover: they were Christians and had determined to build their marriage on Christian principles. Theirs could be described as a Christian marriage.

A day-by-day commitment
What had kept them going 'as smooth as new' for all those years? Peter and Esther had entered into marriage in God's name and they actively trusted God to perfect their marriage by his grace. One day, the youngest of their three sons said to his friends: 'I have never heard my parents disagree or shout at each other. . .' Obviously it did not mean that Peter and

Esther never disagreed or quarrelled. After all, they were two different individuals, each with different hopes and desires. They came from two different backgrounds and, as in any marriage, they had habits that needed changing. But what it meant was that they were careful to handle their quarrels and disagreements away from the children — in private — so that the children never noticed. That type of attitude could only come from hearts completely tuned to Christ; hearts controlled and guided by the Holy Spirit; hearts willing to listen and to obey.

A typical day in Peter and Esther's household always began at about 5.30 a.m. The whole family was up and out into the living room, typically referred to in Africa as 'the parlour'. Some of the very young ones found it hard to keep their eyes open and a few heads would still be nodding when Peter announced the hymn or the chorus. Esther started the singing and by the second or third verse most eyes and heads were clear. The day was committed to the Lord in prayer and other requests were laid before him. Peter or Esther would pray and they also encouraged the children to lead in prayers now and then.

Then they would quickly dress up in preparation for the early morning meeting in church. By this time the church bell was calling the members to prayer. This was and still is a common thing in the African village. While Peter and Esther and perhaps the oldest son went to the church for the early morning prayer meeting, the other children did their morning chores.

Then, at the close of day, after supper, the family gathered again for a longer time of hymn-singing, Bible reading and teaching from the Bible, followed by prayers. Peter, as head of the house, led the family devotions. They all learnt from the Bible and Peter and Esther used its teaching to guide and correct their children. Their family was Christ-centred and typical of many of the first-generation African Christians.

Peter and Esther always did everything together and were

of one mind. They took decisions together, ate together, strolled out together, went to church together and shared the same bedroom. In African terms that meant a lot in those days. Their unity illustrated the Bible's teaching on marriage: 'For this reason a man will leave his father and mother and be united to his wife and they will become one flesh. . .' They enjoyed God's guidance and a oneness in their marriage relationship which they kept up long after the children had grown up and left home.

In all their years of marriage, they went through thick and thin together and were a support to each other. Now Peter is dead and Esther is a widow. Though over eighty years old, you can still see love and concern and that 'godly nature' in her. The children, all happily married, are now looking after Esther.

Peter and Esther were a first-generation Christian couple whose marriage showed that God is faithful to what he has promised in the Bible. But although things have changed and African society has undergone a violent upheaval, Christians today can prove, as Peter and Esther did in years gone by, that Jesus Christ, the person on whom their marriage is founded, is 'the same yesterday, today and forever'.

A Christian marriage of today

Tim and Felicia are in their thirties. They were educated in the United States and have returned to live in Africa. They are highly-placed, which in African terms means they have good jobs, a good flat with modern conveniences in the city, a car and well-placed friends. Despite all the differences — in education, material wealth, life-style — their family is a near mirror of Peter and Esther's family of bygone days. Why? They are Christians. There may not be the early morning church bell summoning people to prayers, the pace of life has more than doubled, and permissiveness has set in, yet Tim and Felicia's three boys exhibit such lovely characters that one is forced to wonder why. Their family life is centred on Jesus Christ and his teachings.

From observation and investigation, I discovered that though they do not start the day at 5.30a.m. like Peter and Esther, they give God his rightful place and honour in their lives and in their home. As it was for Peter and Esther, everything is discussed and agreed on together. Tim knows and maintains he is the head of the home, but Felicia is not trampled upon. There are no ugly scenes and even if there are disagreements they are never in front of the children.

I remember sitting in their home one day, watching Felicia give instructions to their two teenage boys about washing-up and so on. These boys were so unlike the typical teenage boys of most non-Christian well-placed Africans. I was astonished when they cheerfully got up and went to the task.

'Do your boys always do this for you?' I was forced to ask. Felicia smiled and replied, 'I just thank the Lord for my boys. They are simply marvellous.'

Love is the key

The settings and situations may differ but Tim and Felicia represent many present-day African Christians who are showing the world that marriage and family life were set up by God, and that Jesus Christ can and does enable people to live together as husband and wife, lovingly and happily 'till death do us part'.

So what is a Christian marriage? It is a marriage entered into by two Christians with the full knowledge and understanding that God is the author of it. It is a marriage that is being worked at, and is made complete, by following what the Bible teaches. Most people nowadays think that being wedded in church will automatically turn their marriage into a Christian one. What a mistake! In a real Christian marriage, the couple will first of all make sure that their lives are securely anchored in Christ, being prepared to trust and obey him and teaching their children to do the same.

But this does not mean that a Christian marriage is dull and lifeless. I once heard a young African woman who has a very happy marriage and home say, 'The Christian home is a home where each partner can be himself or herself; where all the fences are down; where each partner is accepted for what he or she is because of the love that exists between the two.'

Love therefore is the key — real Christian love. After all, God does not wait for us to be perfect before he can accept us. He receives us *as we are* because of his love for us in Christ and he expects us to do the same to one another. This means that each partner's actions are viewed with sympathy and under-standing and corrected gently in love. Real Christian love is also willing to make sacrifices. So, each partner is ready to sacrifice personal ambitions and aspirations for the smooth running of the home. I can think of Comfort, a young grad-uate, who gave up her job and postponed her further studies because of the children. Also of Mark, another hard-working young man, who turned down a very tempting offer of a job because it meant adjustments which would seriously disrupt his family life.

In a Christian marriage, each partner takes Paul's command in his letter to the Ephesians seriously. He says, 'Wives, submit to your husbands as to the Lord. For the husband is the head of the wife as Christ is the head of the church, his body, of which he is the saviour. . . Husbands, love your wives, just as Christ loved the church and gave himself up for her. . .' We shall consider the implications of these commands fully later in the book.

Christian couples are people just like any other couples, except for one very important factor — they have Jesus Christ and they take him seriously. They are prepared to fight and wage war on anything that will bring disorder or discord to the home. Yet they do not live in paradise; they live in society. They live within a culture which makes its own demands and produces its own dilemmas. Let us now look at some of these.

2

Becoming Husband and Wife

In Western culture, a boy meets a girl and they fall in love. Later, they want to marry and they agree on it. They then tell their parents about it and all is arranged.

In the traditional African culture, a boy thinks he ought to get married, and first tells his father of his wish and intention. Then his situation is vetted to make sure he can support a wife and possibly a family. After that, they start to look for a wife for him.

Details vary from place to place but the tradition is the same. 'The African marries and then falls in love', so the saying goes. The young man who wants to marry may or may not have a say in the choice of his partner. That applies also to the girls. In Africa, it is not a matter for two individuals; you get married to, or you marry into, a family. It is a common practice for a man to approach you and ask for a recommendation for his son. 'I am looking for a wife for my son,' he says. 'Any suggestions?'

There have been variations and changes in some areas and circumstances but the family involvement is still the underlying principle in marriage in Africa. It is possible nowadays for a young man to meet a girl he wants to marry and get her consent. But the process of acquiring her as a wife is carried out by his family. Anything outside these procedures is regarded as an abnormality and is treated as such.

Let us now look at how two families were joined together in a marriage contract by going through the usual cultural process.

Emmanuel and Comfort

Emmanuel is a graduate and now in his late thirties. He finished his university education at twenty-four and worked for some four years. At that time he was ready to get married and able to support a wife and family. He is a Christian and, therefore, knew that he must marry a Christian girl, as the Bible teaches. He was involved in a lot of Christian activities, which enabled him to meet a lot of Christian young girls. He knew that marriage was not to be considered without much prayer and thought, and that he needed to be sure of the Lord's guidance, particularly for the choice. So he prayed and the Lord led him to a young girl who also believed that God wanted them to be married.

They proceeded to inform their people. The boy had to inform his parents; and the girl, her *mother*. This in itself was an advance, for traditionally the girl used to be informed by the mother that suitors were coming with inquiries about her. Although the couple were Christians and believed that it was the will of God that they should marry, they were still Africans and therefore did not want to defy the custom. They knew that the Lord was guiding them and so they expected him to guide them through the customary requirements that had to be met before they could be married. This couple were further encouraged because both sets of parents were Christians as well. In other cases, the going can often be very rough for the young couple concerned. However, things still had to be done in the 'proper' manner.

Emmanuel informed his father and eventually his mother. Now his parents were both satisfied that he was ready for marriage. Then the necessary vetting had to be done to make sure the girl was from a good family. Satisfied, they sent a message to the girl's parents that their son Emmanuel wanted to marry their daughter Comfort. Traditionally, most fathers say no to any initial offers of marriage to their daughter, so Comfort's mother had to put a lot of pressure on her husband to convince him that his objection was unreasonable.

Comfort's mother succeeded, but not before her husband had done his own vetting and was convinced beyond doubt that Emmanuel and his family had no 'blemish'. This vetting is usually done by carrying out a thorough investigation on the family concerned, to be absolutely sure that they have no stain of one type or another, ranging from a bad name to a family history of lunacy or disease — which things are regarded as taboo in Africa. Nowadays, however, the type of thing that will stop a marriage from going ahead are very limited. But still the investigations are religiously carried out.

The first meal

When Comfort's parents were satisfied with Emmanuel and his family, they encouraged Emmanuel's people to come and 'knock on their door', which meant they should pay a formal visit with a few gifts and drinks, to make a formal request for Comfort. They say in some areas, 'Drinks precede any talks.' From this time, Emmanuel played no further major part in the whole process of procuring Comfort as wife, except accompanying his people during all the required visits. Comfort too was to be seen and not heard, except when asked to speak or act. During that first formal visit to Comfort's parents, a day was fixed for Emmanuel's extended family to go to meet Comfort's own people. This would be their formal engagement party, a feast, the size of which is determined by the size and affluence of the two families. This turned out to be one of those big feasts.

On the appointed day, there was a very large crowd of people — brothers, sisters, uncles, aunts, cousins both close and distant, friends and well-wishers from both sides. People started gathering in the early afternoon, and by mid-afternoon the ceremony formally started. It lasted well into the night — the unwritten rule is that you do not rush or hurry over anything. It was a big day for everyone. There was plenty of food and drink, even for those not actually invited but who just joined in. This was normal since no tickets were required and all who chanced by were welcome.

Before the merriment entered into full swing, Comfort was sent for by her family, mostly the men who sat out in the open space in a sort of semi-circle, facing the visitors who also sat in a group. There was a hush when she arrived because something very vital was about to take place. Comfort was going to point out to her large family and to all present who her intended husband was.

'Comfort,' began the oldest man from her family, 'we have all been summoned here by your parents and they have told us that you are intending to leave us. It is indeed a happy loss. We cannot marry you, my daughter, and so, we cannot stand in your way. But we will be happy if you will show us who this bold and daring fellow is.'

Then he handed her a cup of palm-wine, quickly filled and brought over by one of the young men beside him. Comfort shyly pretended to sip a bit from the cup and then went over to where the visitors were sitting until she came to Emmanuel. She knelt down and handed the cup to him.

There was an uproar of clapping and giggles and shouts of 'You have good taste' and 'What a prince charming!' Amidst the cheering and clapping she quickly slipped back into the house and disappeared. Now she was no longer needed, because she had accomplished the one and only task for that day which had any direct bearing on her marriage to Emmanuel.

This 'introduction' is an important part of the process. It differs from place to place, but the basic idea remains the same. In some places, the introduction is reversed. The boy arrives with his family and they are happily received by the girl's family. He is at once formally introduced and is known by everyone present. Then, at an agreed period during the celebration, the girl is introduced in a most amusingly dramatic manner — rather reminiscent of the expensive joke pulled on Jacob by his father-in-law Laban, described in the

Bible in the Book of Genesis. There, the custom was to present the veiled bride to the bridegroom at midnight. So, they presented Leah to Jacob instead of his beloved Rachel.

In Africa, the presentation of the veiled girl is done during the course of the celebration. It is not just to the bridegroom-to-be but to his entire family present. The amusement comes from the fact that intentional mistakes are made by the girl's family, first presenting a couple of veiled 'fakes' who will promptly be rejected by the boy's family with amusing comments. In the end, the 'queen' is presented amidst clapping and a standing ovation. After this, the celebration continues, and the girl who had obviously been absent can now join in if she wants to.

Family gifts

Back to Emmanuel and Comfort. Inside the house were piled the gifts required from Emmanuel's family: heads of dried tobacco, pots of wine and some cartons of lager beer; bottles of hot drinks, packets of cigarettes, clothes, shoes, some stockfish and other smaller items. These days it is not uncommon to see wrist-watches included.

At the time when Emmanuel and Comfort were getting married, Christians did not have as strong a voice as they do now, so neither they nor their parents could do anything much about some of the items on the list. Nowadays it is different. Christians are campaigning strongly and rather successfully about being allowed not to give tobacco or alcohol because of how they may affect their Christian witness within their cultural setting. They would rather bring soft drinks and extra cash. Much, however, depends on the girl's family accepting (or being persuaded to accept) the arrangement.

All these gifts were to be handed out to different categories of people within the larger family, like all wives, young girls within the family, all men, and so on. There were also fixed sums of money specifically meant for different sets of people like mother, uncles, aunts, different age groups within the larger family. The distribution of these items would take place in later days. But for today, it was feasting and merriment for everyone, guest and host alike, with Comfort's parents providing the goodies.

The bride-price

We are told that in some parts of Africa, in times gone by, the feasting would go on into the night. And then, at a signal, a hush would be called and a bride-price determined. Because the guests sat on one side and the hosts sat opposite, it was like a house of debate.

A spokesman from the visiting team would rise and demand from the home team what price they were asking on their daughter's head. A fantastic price would be announced by the spokesman from the home team, after listing their daughter's qualities, ranging from personal beauty to strength to bear children, judging from the number her mother bore for the father. This was of the utmost importance because the strongest reason for an African marriage was for the bearing of children. The reply from the hosts then opened up a whole barrage of arguments and fierce debate and haggling, till a fair price was reached and agreed upon by all. It was like the sale of any important commodity — except that this was the most highly-priced of all commodities.

In some other areas of Africa, when the bride-price was agreed, a deposit was paid, and the young girl was then taken home and 'tried' for fertility. She had to be actually pregnant before the entire bride-price was paid. This allowed her to be 'returned' without landing her family in debt, for it was the custom that if a 'trial' or indeed a concluded marriage failed, the girl was brought back to her parents and they had to pay back all they had taken from the in-laws.

Where Emmanuel's and Comfort's people live, though, the practice was to agree on the bride-price, finish the feasting and pay off the price, except for a small amount, which helped prevent the situation degenerating into an outright 'sale' of a human being. That little debt, which by the way is never settled, also justified mutual interest between the in-laws, and gave the father-in-law a slight edge over his son-in-law. The bride-price was not always in money. It could be paid in cows or any other agreed currency. And in some areas it might be a mere token amount in actual money, in addition to goods and materials.

By the time Emmanuel and Comfort were getting married, however, money had become the medium of buying and selling and so the bride-price was taken in money. Also, the old custom of negotiating a bride-price through haggling and debate had become very unpopular. Many parents resented the idea of bargaining over their daughter. Instead, they would ask the visiting family to give anything they felt like giving. The visiting family would then confer among themselves and offer something reasonable. The details have therefore changed, but the principles still remain.

In other cases, parents make it even simpler for all concerned, having a standard list of all customary requirements, including the bride-price, for every girl in the family going into marriage. This list is handed to the visiting family who set about procuring everything on it. During the ceremonies, the bride-price is simply handed over at the appropriate time and the feasting continues without much interruption. Sometimes, no money is demanded for the bride-price. The son-in-law-to-be is simply asked to pledge responsibility for the education of one child in the family from Primary to University level. Such pledges, though mostly unwritten, are completely binding; and in Africa, where education is the responsibility of parents rather than government, it is a huge commitment. Mostly people would prefer to pay the bride-price once and for all. This kind of 'modern' bride-price shows that the culture is not as rigid and static as people at times think.

But Comfort's father took all this a stage further. He was an African Christian who did not reject or break away from the rich culture, but wanted to see it refined to a point of real meaning and beauty. He did not want to have bride-price discussed at all and he assured his family that all was going to be fine. Comfort was not going to be given away for nothing. And so, as the feasting and merriment were in progress, he took Emmanuel in and asked him how much he proposed to give him for his daughter Comfort. Emmanuel simply handed him the modest sum of money he had come along with. That ended the matter and no one knew how much was given, nor did anyone discuss the issue. Normally, the bride-price goes to the father of the girl. This way of settling the bride-price was different, but it was acceptable to both families. Every other thing went on smoothly. There were speeches and jokes and people thoroughly enjoyed themselves.

Visiting his family

As the day wore on and it was just beginning to get dark, Emmanuel's family rose to leave. There were a few more exchanges of greetings of gratitude for the presents brought, and the wonderful hospitality and the good food received. Amidst all that, the oldest member from Emmanuel's family cleared his throat and once more there was a momentary hush.

'Our people,' he began with a little smile on his lips, 'we are now standing; and though our eyes are on the road, we stand rooted on the spot. When our hosts want us to go, we will leave.'

Such flowery expressions are very common features in African communications. Those who have that art of expression are always in high demand on special occasions. The hosts understood what he meant and explained that their daughter was quickly preparing to leave with them. The custom required Comfort to accompany Emmanuel and his people home to spend four days. This is an opportunity for any would-be bride to make sure that she really likes the husband's family set-up and is happy to spend the rest of her life with them. The husband's family, in their turn, are supposed to observe the would-be wife in their own setting and then make up their minds.

Comfort got some things together in a small suitcase and exchanged a few tearful farewells with her younger brother and sisters. Her parents stood outside, flanked by other relations as they tried to keep up a smiling face while saying their own 'farewell'. From her parents' faces it was obvious that they were both happy and sad to see her go — happy because it is a good and welcome thing for one's daughter to get married; and sad because they were very fond of her. But she was not being lost to them. After all, they were gaining a new 'son' in Emmanuel and, if there was no hitch as they expected, the whole marriage contract would soon be concluded and they would see their daughter frequently, with their new son-in-law.

After a few more exchanges of farewell, the party left. At this stage, nothing had been concluded, even though the bride-price had been paid. Comfort would spend her four days and come back with her verdict, which would pave the way for the third and more important visit from Emmanuel's family. If the girl was impressed and happy, her parents would invite the boy's family to come to have the marriage contract sealed.

Because Emmanuel and Comfort were Christians, the whole process was a mere formality, satisfying the cultural requirement. All the same, Comfort liked what she saw during her very brief stay. She too impressed Emmanuel's parents and relations who immediately accepted her. There was no problem then when her parents sent a message to Emmanuel's parents setting out the date for the third visit — this time to seal the marriage contract.

The third visit

This third visit was to be an important ceremony attended by the entire family, similar to the previous gathering, except for the bride-price issue and the introduction of the would-be husband. The merriment, dancing, and all the talk and jokes were similar. But one distinguishing feature was that this time

Emmanuel's family brought along, amongst other gifts, a goat.

In this part of Africa, the goat plays a very important part as a symbol of agreement. Translated into Western thought, and in business terms, it is comparable to a final signature on a contract, or a seal. In this third visit, there are two meal-times. The first meal is soon after the party arrives. Then there is a session when elaborate entertainment is provided, accompanied by music and dancing. Later in the day, there is another meal. This is a kind of farewell meal, because, after the meal and as drinking continues, people are free to leave if they have to.

During the second meal-time, the goat brought along by Emmanuel's family and handed over on arrival, was shared by all. Some portions of the meat were given out to different people in both families, who by custom should receive a share. Emmanuel, for example, received the neck portion, on behalf of the children that he and Comfort would bring into the world. This underlines the importance attached to children by most African cultures, and also demonstrated the firm belief that the union would be 'fruitful'. Just as the killing of goats in deals and sales denotes the sealing of the agreement between two parties in the contract, so it was the same in this case. The marriage deal was sealed. Comfort was married.

Traditionally, Comfort would accompany her new family home again for a period of eight days, at the end of which she would return home to her own family and then get ready for a final departure. Once the whole process had reached this third-visit stage to seal the marriage contract, there could be no going back on it. That would constitute formal divorce. If for any reason the girl did not like her new family or vice versa the whole thing could be abandoned earlier, after her four-day stay with the family, for example. That would not be regarded as divorce, but as an attempt that didn't succeed. The bride-price or deposit would simply be handed back and the whole matter dropped.

Everything had gone smoothly for Comfort and Emmanuel. Comfort was now Emmanuel's wife as far as her parents were concerned, and parental influence was now transferred to Emmanuel's parents. But Emmanuel and Comfort, together with their parents, were Christians. And so they did not regard the matter as finished. Emmanuel's parents had satisfied the cultural requirement by formally asking for Comfort's hand in marriage to their son, through her family. But for Christians, there is one final stage.

Setting up the home

If Emmanuel and Comfort were not Christians, they could go ahead and set up a home. The pattern goes like this: on an appointed day, a selected group of people from among the older folks in the bride's family, as well as a large number of all the unmarried daughters of that family, accompany the bride's parents as they take her to her new home. The entourage arrives in style with lots of dancing to music supplied by the young damsels, singing special songs for that occasion. Again, there is lots to eat and drink. The bride is formally handed over to her new family and her own family are expected to make gifts to her, comprising all the things that she needs to set up a new home. It is said that sometimes the quantity of things given depends on how much the in-laws paid as bride-price. As there are no binding laws controlling this, the gifts often become a status symbol. If the girl's parents are rich or even just well-to-do, they show it off by giving more than the bride-price could ever have purchased.

The vital thing here is that the newly married wife has been brought home and that in turn means that her family, who are now in-laws, have come to know the 'way to their in-law's home' as they put it. The ceremony usually lasts for a fairly long time and this time the boy's family provide the goodies. This occasion is the nearest equivalent of a 'wedding' in Western culture or Christian practice.

Comfort was not 'brought home' in the traditional way.

For Christians, a new system has been adopted for this final announcement. Emmanuel and Comfort would wed in church.

The Christian difference

Let us now look more closely at the Christian view of marriage, and how this relates to the situation of Emmanuel and Comfort. The Bible clearly states the universal law of God regarding marriage: 'Therefore a man leaves his father and his mother and cleaves to his wife and they become one flesh.' The Jews, through whom this universal law was passed on to the world, have their own marriage customs. For instance, we understand that the final ceremony itself lasted for seven days and that the home going of the couple always took place at night. God laid down the universal principle, but the details differed from culture to culture. But each time it involves an agreement, a public announcement, and a 'leaving and cleaving' and the man and the woman become one unit.

The African Christian, therefore, finds no problem in his method of obtaining an agreement, and the public announcement, as his culture requires. But he wants to make sure that he goes along with God at the end of the day. He goes through all the cultural requirements and follows the procedure, as long as there are no contradictions at any stage between them and his Christianity. Having procured a wife, he then presents the whole situation to God as an additional Christian practice.

The teaching of Jesus, 'Give to Caesar that which is Caesar's, and to God that which is God's', seems to apply here. This was Jesus' answer when presented with the practical question of whether it was lawful for the Jews under Roman rule to pay taxes to Caesar, the Roman Emperor. It was obvious that the questioners were trying to catch him out. They thought that whichever way he answered, he would offend someone. An unqualified 'yes' would mean that he supported the Roman overlords in their colonization policy, and so could not justify his claim that he had come to help his people; but a 'no' would bring an accusation from the Romans that he was encouraging rebellion against authority. But then came the perfect answer.

'Why do you put me to the test, you hypocrites?' he charged back. 'Show me the money for the tax.'

And they brought him a coin.

Then came the vital question, 'Whose likeness and inscription is this?'

'Caesar's,' came the answer.

Then Jesus laid down the divine principle. 'Give to Caesar that which is Caesar's, and to God that which is God's.'

The African Christian has always applied this principle rightly to his marriage situation. The question is always, 'What is the cultural requirement?' As long as it does not go against Christian teaching and practice, the cultural requirement should be met. Up to the point of concluding the marriage contract, Emmanuel's family had no problem. They were simply giving to 'Caesar' the things that belonged to 'Caesar'. They had fulfilled all the requirements and received Comfort as Emmanuel's wife. Or had they? This is the area that presents a dilemma for young African Christians getting married.

Waiting for the wedding

Emmanuel and Comfort were as good as married. In the eyes of many people, culturally speaking, they were: but as far as the Christian community was concerned, they were not married because they had not wedded in church. They were simply engaged. Even though Comfort was now allowed to visit and stay at Emmanuel's home for as long as she wanted, they were not allowed to sleep together or set up a family of their own. The Christian commitment of the family was strong, and the young couple was chaperoned.

Weddings are often very big occasions and therefore need careful planning. So, it is possible for the time-gap between acquiring a wife and the wedding to be fairly lengthy. This produces problems. Because it is a family affair, the young ones may not necessarily have a final say in their wedding.

Until recently, the whole thing was planned and carried out by the family. So, the 'engaged couple' had to wait for as long as they were required to wait. Often they were strained because they were left in a situation of 'married' but yet not married. The Christian community is quite strict on the couples staying apart until the wedding day. Christians consider any physical meeting as sex before marriage and an offending couple is often disciplined.

Emmanuel and Comfort had only six months to wait. For them there was no strain at all because they had natural reasons to be separated. Emmanuel was working elsewhere and Comfort still had college to finish and so was on campus. They only made trips home for the ceremonies. And as long as school was on, Emmanuel wrote and visited his darling at school. When the school term ended, Comfort travelled home to Emmanuel's family. From there, she visited her own family. That was the situation. She had been procured by Emmanuel's family for Emmanuel, but was not handed over to him yet. As they were committed Christians, the chaperoning arrangement and understanding worked out well. Others are sometimes not so well arranged and ugly situations may develop.

A memorable day

After six months the wedding arrangements had been finalized and cards distributed. This wedding would be like any other wedding in the 'Christian' Western world – a registration with the Marriage Registry for state records, followed by a wedding service. But the difference is in the reception. These are always social events for Africans.

Cards are distributed to invite specially the people who necessarily should be there. Most often the families of the boy and the girl are not supposed to be given cards. It is their thing and so they should be there as of right. Cards are for others far and near. It is often impossible to put a figure on the crowd expected. You simply work on estimates. But the lovely thing is, as in every other arrangement involving ceremonies and feasts, the African naturally makes over-estimations. There must always be left-overs. Even if you estimated three hundred coming for the wedding, you make provision for four hundred. In most cases the extra provision is taken up because in weddings, everybody is welcome. Again, it is a collective responsibility for the family hosting the wedding. Most often, the boy's family takes the wedding responsibility. But in certain other areas, it is the girl's family. Whatever arrangement is agreed, the wedding itself for the Christian takes the same pattern. It is a big opportunity for feasting.

For Emmanuel and Comfort, it was a memorable day. People came from far and near. Some of Emmanuel's colleagues as well as Comfort's school-mates travelled very long distances to attend. Many hours are often spent in wedding ceremonies and that is why real meals are very important features. That was the case for Emmanuel and Comfort.

There were lots of gifts from friends and well-wishers, but more important, there was that special home-going gift from Comfort's family. Comfort's parents wanted to make their daughter feel good and proud and so they presented her with all that one could ever need to set up a new home. She was indeed proud of her parents. And her parents were not alone in this practice. Nowadays, it is a common thing to be given all 'home property' plus a car or even a house, as happened not too long ago. This is a carry-over from the cultural practice-made-Christian — no conflict, no problems!

Overcoming cultural difficulties

Anthropologists tell us that no culture is static and that each cultural pattern or practice is often subject to change. The African culture is no exception. As Christianity emerged, the African culture began to experience modifications, adaptations and some changes. So, the marriage customs too have undergone a lot of alterations and modifications. Some of these are easily acceptable, others bring about conflicts; but as long as the Bible is the standard, the African Christian should be prepared and happy to face these situations. There are areas in the traditional culture where Christians have found a new way through, without producing conflicts.

Of all the customary requirements for marriage, gifts of tobacco and alcohol pose the biggest problem. For some African Christians, alcoholic drink is a taboo because of the social problems caused by alcoholism. For such people, conflicts always develop when the marriage custom demands that alcoholic drinks must be presented as a requirement for procuring the hand of a girl in marriage from her family. Initially, this problem was very difficult to solve, but now compromises have been found in different areas.

For the Christian who is trying to marry another Christian girl whose family is not Christian, money has been accepted in place of alcoholic drinks. Invariably the drinks are bought and distributed by the girl's family with the money provided by the boy. But the understanding is that he is not the one buying and giving it and so his conscience is clear.

Others have been able, as a group of Christians in an area, to convince people around them that producing alcohol during negotiations, directly or indirectly, is totally objectionable. From my own experience and reports from others, it seems that customs have been relaxed for them and they have been able to conclude some agreements without giving any type of alcoholic drink.

To other more mature and accommodating Christians, there is a fairly simple compromise. Whatever the people demand, they give, on the understanding that they will not themselves partake of it. So, they will give the required quantity of alcoholic drinks to the girl's family because that is what her family, at their own level, understand and accept. To such people, they are simply 'giving Caesar what is Caesar's'. Tobacco is treated along the same lines. When both parties engaged in the marriage issue are indeed Christians in the larger family sense, things are a lot easier, but this is not typical.

On the other hand, any practice that is involved in, or appears to be involved in, pagan worship is rejected outright by Christians. An example of this is the offering of things like drinks or other items of food to either the departed forebears or gods. Instead, they insist on Christian prayers. In traditional culture, many things are said and gratitude is expressed to ancestors for blessings of all sorts. Now instead, prayers (lengthy ones sometimes) are said and God is given the glory for all blessings. In all cases I know of, the custom has been altered. Christians make sure that everything they do is true to the Bible. And so the Christian faith is helping to bring about changes.

Areas of conflict

But there still remain areas of conflict between Christianity and culture. In the real cultural practice, the family, headed by the father, chooses a wife for the son or approves a husband for the girl. Christian young men and women have been resisting and fighting this aspect of culture because, in the end, even though the couple remains part of the larger family, it is still the two individuals that are married. It is true that Africans marry from or into families but there is a saying that 'ours is ours, but mine is mine'. So, most young people refuse to be chosen for. They make the choice themselves and, except in very extreme circumstances, this will be approved by the family, after the necessary vetting. Culture has given way to the strong wishes of the young.

This personal choice idea which is practised everywhere now, by non-Christians and Christians alike, began when a few Christians resisted the idea of being chosen for. Family loyalty remains, but the conflict of choice has produced this new freedom. This right to choose is born out of Christian freedom which comes only from strong Christian convictions.

Amos was a committed Christian, but his family had a nominal Christianity. He was the first male child of the family and therefore, in his late twenties, was under constant pressure to get married. The family went ahead after some time to choose a girl for him. She came from a good family, was pretty and, what was more, from her family records and evaluation, she would make a very good wife and should be able to bear many children.

These very positive considerations made her the ideal choice for their son Amos. At this time, Amos was studying overseas. Amos's family wanted to procure the girl and send her over so that the two could get married overseas and start a home. After all, Amos was overdue for starting a family and, being a first son, should start a family as a matter of urgency in order to continue the family line. Amos, who was not consulted in the whole affair, rejected the choice and clearly stated that he should be allowed to choose for himself the girl he was going to spend the rest of his life with. 'And,' said Amos, 'the girl must be a Christian.'

However, his family did not take him seriously and went ahead to procure the girl who herself was excited at the prospect of going overseas. Then Amos travelled home to make his stand known. He had never seen the girl before and was not prepared to enter into a marriage of that nature. The family had acquired the girl and Amos would not have her. Now, she remains in her family waiting for the final home-going, while Amos still remains unmarried.

This conflict has nearly split Amos's family, but Amos is sticking to his guns. He still remains loyal to his family, but will not budge from his stand on this issue. It has caused some family strain, but it is a 'welcome' strain to him. Some critics would term him a fanatic, but he is faithful to his Christian convictions. Paul, in his second letter to the Corinthians, warns Christians: 'Do not be mismated with unbelievers. For what partnership have righteousness and iniquity? Or what fellowship has light with darkness? What accord has Christ with Belial? Or what has a believer in common with an unbeliever? What agreement has the temple of God with idols?' The predictable outcome of the stalemate is that Amos's family, though ashamed of being let down by their son, will eventually pipe down. It has happened before in the case of another young man who, after two years of stalemate, was allowed to make his own choice. The same will be the case here in the end.

This freedom to choose produces a different kind of conflict at times. It happens when a Christian young man or woman prayerfully discovers who the Lord wants them to marry, and duly informs their parents. But the choice is rejected after some vetting, on cultural grounds which the Christian does not accept as a genuine reason.

Sam was convinced the Lord was leading him to marry Esther. He prayerfully approached Esther who, after praying about it for some time, accepted the offer. Their parents were informed. But the girl's family rejected her choice on the grounds that the distance between her village and Sam's village was too much. They tried to discourage Esther but found her very adamant. They tried to put Sam off by demanding a very highly inflated figure as dowry, but Sam's father, who was wealthy, called their bluff. He paid the outstanding dowry and procured Esther for his son.

Esther felt humiliated by the unreasonableness of her family, and her family in turn became ashamed of themselves and regretted their actions. But nothing could be done about it. The relationship between the in-laws was strained in the process too, though time would eventually heal the strain.

Abel and Juliet had the same conflict. They were sure the Lord wanted them to marry, but Juliet's family would not have him as a son-in-law. Several delegations approached them, including the local church dignitaries. But they remained adamant. After about one year, Abel and Juliet were advised and supported by the Christian community to go ahead and wed without any native law and customs or parental consent or approval. Subsequently, Juliet's people piped down, partly because they observed through their 'spies' that their daughter was very happy, and because the Lord had blessed their marriage with a baby. They then gave the go-ahead for the customary formalities to be carried out.

When Joy's family would not allow Reuben's people to visit them on the grounds that Reuben did not measure up to the standard or expectations regarding a son-in-law, she stubbornly held her ground and would not yield to any pressure. Her resolve paid off, her wishes were granted, and the cultural formalities were arranged.

In all these three cases, the couples were sure that it was the Lord's leading and they could not allow anything, culture or no culture, to deter them from their goals. In all three cases, the families gave in to strong Christian determination and conviction.

In some areas, it used to be the common cultural practice for the wife-to-be to be 'proved' before finally 'wedded' by the prospective husband. This was to make sure she could actually bear children. Again, through changes brought about by the influence of Christianity, the practice is phasing out. I remember being present at a conference where there was a heated discussion over the issue by the young people. It became clear that over 90 per cent of the Christians present rejected this practice. While culture permits it, the Bible condemns fornication − sex before marriage.

The custom seemed more like the sale of a work-horse or mule than getting married to a life-partner. Having children was put in its right perspective. Whereas the culture was seeing it as the most important reason for marriage, Christians were seeing it as a blessing that accompanied marriage. Marriage is not just for bearing children. Marriage is love and companionship. When writing to the Christians at Ephesus, Paul says, 'For this reason a man shall leave his father and mother, and be joined to his wife, and the two shall become one flesh.'

At the end of the meeting one young man came up to me and said, 'I have never thought of this practice in this way. For the first time I realize that one can easily disobey the Lord because of culture. If my fiancée could not get pregnant and I therefore refused to take her as my wife what I had done would constitute fornication.'

'Yes,' I replied.

'And even if she did get pregnant and I married her, I would live with a guilty conscience,' he continued.

'Exactly,' I said.

'So either way it is wrong?'

'Precisely,' I confirmed.

He looked at me with a smile and said, 'Praise God.'

I patted him on the back as he turned to leave. I rejoiced because the truth of the gospel was producing good results. Culture is being refined and made pure by the Creator of all cultures. What is cultural or customary may not necessarily be good when put side by side with the Word of God.

Keeping the good, changing the bad

For the African Christian, then, compromises help to smooth out difficult situations but conflicts produce change. For the majority of Christians, the idea of choosing a wife for anybody or accepting a husband on somebody's recommendation has been stopped. So too are other practices to do with pagan worship. There are still other areas where change or further alterations are needed. The long gap between the customary 'marriage' of the couple and the actual Christian wedding, as was stated earlier, produces a strain for the young 'engaged' couple. In all respects, customarily speaking, they are married; but Christians see them as merely engaged. In many instances, ugly situations have cropped up when the girl has become pregnant because of lack of self-control caused by weak chaperoning. In such cases a quick wedding is always arranged, but the stigma remains. No matter if a blind eye is turned to it — a disgrace always remains a disgrace.

To avoid such situations, many families have started delaying the final visit to the girl's family, which will release her to them, until a few weeks or at times a few days before the wedding. That works perfectly. With such changes, therefore, Christianity is helping to refine African marriage customs while retaining all of their richness and splendour.

3

New Patterns of Marriage

A new wave of marriage practice has begun to emerge among many educated people in Africa today. This is marriage without family consent or blessing. It has been brought about by the ease of travel and international contact and is thought by many to be a result of direct influence of the 'Christian-Western' culture. Indeed, progress and education came with the advent of Christianity and Africans who are taking this new approach are the educated, those who have travelled to the West.

So far, it has not gained much ground, or any approval, but the practice is on the increase in different areas. It has not in any way become accepted cultural practice, but rather springs from an over-reaction by some well-travelled and educated people to what they see as an inhibiting and narrow-minded marriage custom. Not all educated people share this view, but for some the practice is becoming popular.

Akpan and Mfun

Akpan and Mfun met while studying in the United Kingdom. They fell in love and were convinced that they suited each other in marriage. Being Christians, they spent some weeks praying over the issue until they were really certain it was God's will for them to marry. They came from two different sections of the same tribe in Africa with slight differences in marriage custom. Nevertheless, they boldly travelled home to their people during one long vacation and had things discussed and sorted out.

As a result, the customary requirements were met fairly

quickly, taking into account the fact that they had only a short time at home. Their sincerity and determination were supported by their families and they returned to the United Kingdom and had their wedding. They were happy, their families were satisfied and also happy. These were practising Christians and by their actions they showed their families that they still held the culture in the highest possible esteem.

Victor and Hannah

Some others, however, hide under the cloak of Christianity and defy their culture. They challenge the accepted way of doing things. Perhaps they read the stories in books written in the West for Western culture, or they get their ideas from movies; they then proceed to try it out to test the society. This, they say, may be the best way of bringing a change. 'We do not have to wait till the awareness slowly evolves,' they argue. At least, that tends to be the philosophy behind such actions.

In the late sixties, Victor, a young and handsome final-year engineering student, fell in love with Hannah, an equally beautiful and musically talented young lady, who still had two sessions to do at the university. They were very much in love − or so they thought. They knew that most families had now come to the stage when they would not mind their children discovering life-partners for themselves. They equally knew that respect for their culture required them to tell their parents at once if they were seriously thinking of getting married. But perhaps they feared that they could not possibly convince their families to let them get married while still at school − not in those days.

So they proceeded to go to the Marriage Registry, grabbed two of their close friends as witnesses, and got married. In their country anyone above the age of consent could get married according to the law. They had the twenty-one days' marriage notices for possible objections stuck up at the Registrar's office notice-board, some one hundred miles away from their villages. Thus in a rather 'smooth' and unperturbed manner, they got married while on campus — just the way it happened in the Western movies they were fond of watching. Later they proceeded to inform their families — not of their intention to get married, but of the fact that they were already married.

Ebe and Lulu

Lulu's case was quite different. It was not on campus and she was not a university student, but an office-worker. She was always meeting this rather athletic-looking young man at the place where she regularly went to buy her snacks. After several meetings and several side-glances, they formally 'broke the ice' and discovered that each had been 'dying to meet' the other — which explained the regularity in snack-buying at the same joint.

Soon they began visiting each other frequently. As in most big cities, there were no parental or family checks on their movements. Before too long, cooking for Ebe became a regular Saturday event which Lulu quite enjoyed. At first, Sundays were not for visits since Lulu sang in her church choir. Whether she actually understood the implications of Christianity and church is quite a different matter. As a young girl at home she had sung in the choir and since coming to the city to work after finishing her secondary education, she had kept up the habit.

Lulu lived with her uncle in the city when she first arrived, but a few months before she actually met Ebe, she had moved over to her own one-room 'house'. It was the in-thing in those days. Such dwellings were actually single-floor bungalows carved into between six and eight rooms and rented out to young office-workers. A large curtain down the middle of the room converted it into two apartments — the 'bedroom' behind the curtain and the 'living room' before the curtain. The living room had space for one or two chairs, and in the corner stood the 'wardrobe' — like the goal-post-shaped stands seen in departmental stores. Everyday and work clothes were often hung out in this section of the 'house' while the Sunday-bests and party dresses were neatly tucked away in a box, carefully concealed in the corner of the 'bedroom' or under the bed.

Also behind the curtain was the pantry and kitchen cupboard. Some people actually did their cooking behind the curtain, which tended to leave a mixed odour hanging over the whole room. But Lulu used the general kitchen which served all six occupants of the bungalow, along with the common conveniences. This was a typical working-class dwelling in the cities in those days. Some had better dwellings of two separate rooms with a connecting door. They were a more privileged set of the working class in higher positions − and that was what Ebe was.

To start with, Lulu was content to have Ebe visit her on Saturdays for her lovely cooking. She might not perhaps have fallen for it had she not accepted a very persuasive invitation from Ebe to visit him for just a few hours after her morning service. Ebe never really went to church. His family was not pagan but they were not committed Christians either. He had been through the grill of church primary and secondary schools before attending a government technical college where it was not compulsory to attend worship services. It was then that he opted out and had stayed out ever since, except for occasionally accompanying friends for baptisms of their babies and such-like.

Lulu arrived according to plan and was quite impressed by Ebe's living conditions and the whole atmosphere. She missed her evening service that Sunday and was to miss it for many other Sundays. Their visits became more frequent and Ebe often took her out to the cinema and once to a dance hall. She was really infatuated. He was treating her very kindly and he was so strong and handsome. She lost her somewhat steady form. They started taking liberties. Tragedy struck − she was pregnant!

This was a tragedy because it was a stigma on her and her

family – pregnancy outside wedlock. Something must be done. They had no immoral courage to take out a secret abortion. There was only one way out. Ebe took her to the Marriage Registrar and they got married. Lulu moved in with Ebe. They could not stand the idea of telling their people and they were safe in the city where people were not from one particular village and therefore could not 'press charges'. But, before long, the news filtered home to their village.

There was a stir in their families and Lulu's mother quickly found assistance to travel to the city to sort her daughter out. After all, it may have been only a rumour and not necessarily true. To prove her point, Lulu's mother first went to her daughter's former address – only to be told she had moved. After a long spell of blinking and head-shaking, the young man they had met finally told her guide where Lulu could be found.

Immediately they set off. They arrived there and found Lulu. Africans say that one cannot cover pregnancy with a basket. When the mother saw her daughter, her spirit fell and her knees wobbled. Lulu had darkened her horizon! She had put the plough before the oxen. And *she* would be blamed for her daughter's misbehaviour. Her face became cloudy as she motioned and touched her guide saying, 'Take me home.'

Shock waves

Victor and Hannah's case illustrates a kind of practice which went on and still goes on in places of higher learning both in Africa and amongst Africans overseas. And in the large cities, the likes of Ebe and Lulu can still be found. But does the increasing frequency of these types of marriage union constitute an accepted change of pattern and format? The answer can only be an unqualified *No!*

When Victor and Hannah told their families about their marriage, both sets of parents were shocked and the whole idea was rejected outright. Neither set of parents could call themselves in-laws because nothing had been talked about –

nothing had been agreed and nothing had been entered into. Both Victor and Hannah were simply seen as prodigal and they were treated as such.

In Hannah's family, there was 'mourning', as her mother was overcome by immense grief because her daughter had run after a man 'like a whore'. She had gone without dignity. No ceremonies; no opportunity for her to dance and display her gifts from her son-in-law's family. 'Shame,' exclaimed her mother, 'has sewn a permanent dress for me and I have to put it on.' Her fellow women mourned with her. Hannah's father lost his prestige and honour among his peers, not to talk of the larger family. For all this meant he could not exercise a firm authority over his daughter. This was to remain a spoken, and sometimes unspoken, taunt for him for ever. . . 'Don't you know that man whose educated daughter ran after an unknown man?' That was the sort of remark which would come his way ever after. To any African father, it would be undermining his character and he was not above average.

On the other hand, the reaction from Victor's family was more of an embarrassment spiced with shock. 'How can you dump me in this kind of situation, Victor?' his father asked him. It was unheard of. There was no way he could start going to Hannah's family *now* to ask for their daughter in marriage. His son had already taken what was not his right to take. All Victor's uncles also found this action shocking and very embarrassing — but for one half-wit who thought it a very heroic act and was suggesting that it should be viewed as a portrayal of the family power and chivalry. His rantings were ignored as always. So nothing was done because no one knew what to do. This had never happened before, and so there were no guidelines on how to approach Hannah's family who came from a fairly distant village. And Hannah's family could not approach Victor's family, because it was never done that way. 'Water doesn't flow upstream,' says an African proverb. Women do not seek men's hand in marriage. It is the other way round. So nothing was done.

Falling apart

Hannah's and Victor's marriage did not receive any family blessing or care or support. After six months it broke down. They drifted apart and stopped seeing each other. Victor left university and 'disappeared'. After many months, Hannah managed to get the 'marriage' nullified on grounds of neglect and desertion. After a long tussle and struggle she also managed to be reconciled with her family and she is now remarried in the proper way to someone else. Her family treat the escapade with Victor as if it never happened; a huge dream — or more correctly, a nightmare — that has passed.

Lulu's marriage also broke down. The families did not support such a marriage, either. The child was born and Lulu's mother did not come for the cultural visit to her daughter designed to help her through the first difficult weeks after childbirth. As the reality of their make-shift marriage dawned on them, fences and masks fell and Ebe began ill-treating Lulu, calling her 'cheap and loose'. Lulu sought for a divorce and Ebe did not contest it. They had entered into what was a make-believe marriage. And now it was no longer. But their ending had a sad note. There was a child. According to culture, Ebe took custody of the child while Lulu tried to patch the broken relationship with her family. Africans never reject their children; they accepted her back. But the stories had been too much and she has remained unmarried ever since.

So, Africans have always rejected this type of practice by some educated folks. But not all marriages of this nature have broken down. Some couples are still living together and have become pure town-dwellers, having very little to do with their people. Some families may resign themselves to the situation but will nevertheless not accept it.

As national consciousness gets stronger in many parts of Africa, there is now a greater sense of pride in identifying with our culture. Most Africans today will want to see the culture refined or modified — but never replaced.

4

Growing in Marriage

There is a saying in Africa that bringing out tubers to the farm land is one thing, but being able to plant them is quite another. Most Africans go through the process of acquiring a wife. Christian or non-Christian, the procedure is the same, as we saw earlier. The traditional man sets up his home as soon as the woman is released by her family to his family, while the Christian hangs on a bit until they have taken a church wedding.

The crunch comes when the marriage is actually being worked out in practice. The traditional home takes its pattern from tradition and culture; the Christian home pattern follows some tradition and culture but its real standard or motivating force are the Christian principles drawn from the Bible's authority. These principles are worked out within the cultural setting.

African culture is very rich, particularly in the area of relationships. Larger family ties are very close, as we saw earlier, and people generally are friendly and willing to share responsibility over children. Any child born within the larger family belongs exclusively to the parents in terms of parenthood, but in terms of care and nurture, it belongs to all. Any adult who sees any child committing an offence has a right to discipline that child as his own. Old people as well enjoy the care of the entire family — whether they are close or not.

Within this framework the Christian home makes the most of these positively strong cultural qualities while finding ways to change some less acceptable practices, bringing them in line with a Christian way of life. God does not condemn any culture but he does have a few things to say about tradition.

It may be argued that tradition is born out of the culture and in its turn helps to shape and form culture; but not all traditions are right and fair. That is why at times certain sides to a culture become uncomfortable.

Weighing up the culture

A Christian is ready at all times to weigh tradition and culture against biblical truths and commands because he or she accepts the Bible as the absolute standard, and believes that Jesus Christ is the truth and the life. The so-called deviations of Christians from their culture, for which at times they are challenged, all begin because the Bible disagrees with an accepted tradition which has so much influenced the culture that it is regarded as the culture. It is often very easy for the non-Christian to challenge the Christian on certain issues which have been accepted by a people as part of their culture, even though wicked and unfair in content. And since no culture is static, disagreements and tensions are always bound to be present.

But one thing is certain and sure for the Christian — the Bible. It is his or her book of life. It is a lamp to the feet and a light to the path. It is her book of wisdom. It is his guidance book and it says of marriage:

'Submit to one another out of reverence for Christ. Wives, submit to your husbands as to the Lord. For the husband is the head of the wife as Christ is the head of the church, his body, of which he is the Saviour. Now as the church submits to Christ, so also wives should submit to their husbands in everything.

'Husbands, love your wives, just as Christ loved the church and gave himself up for her to make her holy, cleansing her by the washing with water through the word, and to present her to himself as a radiant church, without stain or wrinkle or any other blemish but holy and blameless. In this same way, husbands ought to love their wives as their own bodies.

'He who loves his wife loves himself. After all, no one ever hated his own body but he feeds and cares for it, just as Christ does the church — for we are members of his body. "For this reason a man will leave his father and mother and will be united to his wife, and the two will become one flesh." This is a profound mystery — but I am talking about Christ and the church. However, each one of you also must love his wife as he loves himself, and the wife must respect her husband.' (Ephesians 5:21–33)

In the Bible there is every provision for a very happy married life for the Christian couple who follow its teaching. But it does not automatically follow that every Christian marriage is problem-free or is very happy. The problems that Christian families have, or the difficulties they experience, often originate from not understanding and obeying the Bible's teaching. We are all human and we can be tempted or put under pressure to step out of line.

Headship and authority in marriage

For the African Christian, there is a temptation to follow tradition which, in some aspects, lays down a one-sided, unbalanced approach to marriage relationships. By African tradition, the husband is the head, the king and emperor and the wife is the subject and the servant. It is true that the Bible says the husband is the head of the house and that wives should be subject to their husbands, but it *equally* says that husbands should love their wives just as Christ loves his church and gave himself up for her. For any understanding Christian, that places a greater burden on the husband to make sacrifices than on the wife — and that is balance.

The Bible says that the wife is a helper fit for the man, but African tradition says the wife is 'an assistant procured to do the chores'. After all, in most cases, a man procures a wife or wives because he can no longer cope with keeping his house and running his business or farm. So a wife is procured to keep house as well as produce children — the fruits of a man's labour. It is a common thing in the traditional African society to describe a man's possessions as consisting of land, farms, big barns, herds, wife or wives and children.

We shall look at some of these traditional concepts and measure them against the Christian ideals and see why and how the African Christian has his or her tensions and conflicts. Firstly, let us look at the traditional concept of authority and headship as shown in two marriages and compare it with the way two Christian couples have worked it out in their own marriages.

In the village: Obi

It was seven o'clock in the morning and Obi, a respectable man of the village, was hanging around in the 'porch' section of his little village house. His neighbour came in, presumably to discuss a few matters relating to village politics. They exchanged greetings and asked of their health and that of their families. Obi politely offered his neighbour a seat and called his wife. She quickly appeared from somewhere inside the house and at once saluted the neighbour with his village title. A good side-look from Obi and a wave of the hand were quite understood by the wife who disappeared, to reappear moments later with 'kola'.

It is often customary to offer 'kola' to someone who comes to your house, however regular or familiar that person might be with you. The 'kola' sometimes is the actual kola nut, a flat-sided, oval-shaped nut from the kola tree that grows in different parts. Other times it may just be something edible like garden fruits, given to someone as an expression of joyful welcome. This was morning, when the kola nut is thought to be most appropriate. Obi's wife did not bring otherwise. She brought the kola nut in a little saucer, placed it before her husband and sat down on a low, square seat by the corner of the room.

Her husband Obi proceeded to announce the arrival of the kola to all and sundry in the room — his wife and his neighbour. His neighbour replied with the acceptable expression: 'Thank you. The king's kola is in the hands of the king.' This meant that Obi should now go ahead and perform the morning's ceremonial call for blessing for the day from the gods, and to call on the ancestral spirits, not just as witnesses to his plea, but also to come and partake of the kola. It is assumed that the spirits of the departed forefathers always gather around each morning for this ceremony. You are not supposed to see them but you have to include them and call them by name during this time.

Obi began to invoke the blessings of the gods, often addressing each particular god by name and asking for a specific aspect of the day. He also made frequent requests for justice from them by asserting some moral dogmas — 'he who says I should not eat from my labours, may he precede me to the land of the spirits,' he said. The little room resounded with the chorus of 'that is it', from his small audience — his wife and his neighbour.

He repeated two or three more of such forthright requests and then cracked the kola nut into its separable lobes. It fell into four pieces and he rejoiced. That was a good number of lobes and that signified the fact that on the whole his pleas were heard and accepted. Five lobes formed the star number and meant a superlative acceptance, while two or three lobes meant that he would have to tread very carefully throughout that whole day.

Obi picked up one piece which he began to chew rather noisily while he gave the saucer to his wife to pass on to the visitor. His wife passed on the saucer to the neighbour who took one piece. She went back to her low seat and picked up one little piece which she began to nibble into rather quietly. She asked the neighbour about the health of his wife and children. She did not ask these questions when the kola-breaking ceremony was going on because one is not supposed to interrupt or cause distraction for as long as it lasted. They spent a few more moments chewing, each engrossed in their thought-worlds. A few more chewings and swallowing and Obi cleared his throat with a momentarily prolonged grunt.

'Welcome,' he said to his neighbour. His wife got her cue, rose from her chair, thanked the two men and wished them a good time together and disappeared again. This is a man's society and the men were ready to confer together. She responded properly and was never seen or heard again until Obi's neighbour rose to leave after about an hour. She only came out to bid him farewell.

It is not difficult to discover whose show it was. It was Obi's show and that morning set the pattern for the whole day. He made his day's programme and he stated his wishes for the day. His wife was expected to make her plans and weave her activities round his programme and to be sure that his plans ran smoothly. That was the way in Obi's part of Africa. Wives are a part and parcel of the 'family locomotive'. The man is the locomotive engine and the wife is the coach drawn by the engine. The authority in the home is purely the man's and that means authority over everybody and everything.

Before leaving the house that morning for the farm, Obi left instructions concerning what should be done, including asking his wife to make sure that food arrived right on time for him and the farm-workers for that day. Obi's wife wasn't going to the farm this time because the type of work being done was only men's work. Men were expected to cut down, burn up and dig up the land ready for the planting of tubers and other vegetable seeds. The men planted the tubers while the women were left to see to the vegetables and other related seeds which were considered too feminine for the men to be concerned with. Women also did the weeding when it was necessary. So Obi gave out the instructions and he expected them all to be carried out. His wife also knew that her master's words were law and order. After all, doesn't the African say that 'each man is a king in his own house'?

Obi's authority is very closely tied to the fact that he is the head of the household. The man is the head and is expected to exert a totalitarian authority over his household. After all, he owns everything in his house. He either acquired them, including his wife, or they were produced there. It may be assumed that because Obi lived in the village, he was more likely to be traditional and act traditionally. But this is a very mistaken assumption.

In the city: John

Let us now look at another example. John traded in all sorts of commodities and lived in the city with his wife and children. He had managed to scrape some education from the primary schools set up by different missionary agencies in Africa. He was every inch a traditional African, except for his name, which he picked up when he began schooling as a youngster. Every morning he left his house in the city to go to his stall in the market-place where he sold his wares. His wife, like Obi's, received instructions every morning as to tasks that must be performed. He was authoritarian; he was bossy. He was the head and owner of the house and his wife was his housewife with every imaginable emphasis on the word 'house'. 'Before I come back,' he would always bellow out, 'let it be that those clothes at that corner are washed and ironed. I have to attend a gathering somewhere in the evening.' He could leave any instruction, shouting it out on his way to work.

The traditional concept of headship and authority therefore is not limited to a village setting. It has little to do with place. It is found within the individual himself. The heart that is not touched by the Spirit of God, not truly converted to Christ, still remains very traditional both in thought and deed, whether in the city or in the village. The same holds true for the Christian. He is not to be found only in the city. He is also there in the village, in his traditional home, but his attitudes and actions are governed by his faith. His ideals and ideas are different from those of the traditional African.

It is sad, however, that there are many Africans today who go to church but are just as traditional as their forefathers. People such as John are found everywhere — city and village alike. They have Christian names; they attend church services on Sundays because it is something to do, or what every other person does; but they have not in truth let Christ come into their lives and change them and make them new. They are not only those with very little education like John, but also very well-educated people who hold key posts in important offices or companies. Some of them even teach in higher education and universities. There are many men and women like that — fully Westernized in looks and appearance but truly tradition- ally African in thought and actions. I know a highly-placed African in his country's public service whose fairly educated wife does not share the same bedroom with him. This was not because they had too much room in their house but because according to him, 'that is the way our people have always done it'. Women and children are classed below the menfolk and it is often debated as to which of the two groups comes first in importance.

For Christians: 'Love your wife'

But what about Peter and Esther? For them it was a different story. Like Obi, Peter lived in the village but his family's lifestyle was quite different from Obi's and many others. This produced a mixture of reactions from other people, ranging from admiration and envy to sheer bewilderment and, in some cases, hostility. Peter and Esther and their children had a distinctive style of a happy and satisfied family life. They were both villagers by birth, and they were born-again Christians — that is, they had committed their lives to Jesus Christ and asked him to be the Lord and Saviour of their lives.

Tradition demands that each man should be head of his

family and have absolute authority but that way was not for Peter. After becoming a Christian and understanding his Bible, he realized that his position as the head of the family was a role appointed by God. Paul, in his letter to the Corinthians, says, 'Now I want you to realize that the head of every man is Christ, and the head of the woman is man, and the head of Christ is God.' Writing to the Ephesians, Paul says: 'The husband is the head of the wife.' As Peter understood this teaching, he realized that 'headship' did not have the idea of superiority, of being 'better' in personal quality or high moral standard and character than the wife. It is a position which God has ordained and which carries its own responsibilities. Peter explains it like this: 'If that had meant otherwise, it would appear that God is superior to Christ; but the Bible clearly shows that both are equal.'

For Peter, headship was not expressed in the way tradition or custom presented it − a system where a man had to work himself up and prove himself by being authoritarian. Headship in Christian marriage meant leadership with full consultation. The Bible says '. . . husbands ought to love their wives as their own bodies. He who loves his wife loves himself.' The effect on Esther of Peter's attitude was to produce a willing submissive attitude. She also had a deep, loving respect for him and felt 'free' in herself. She and most other African Christian women have never had problems with the headship of their husbands over the entire family. After all, it is the accepted African tradition. But the notable difference between them and their non-Christian counterparts is that, while the attitudes of the Christian husbands put their wives at a considerable ease, non-Christian husbands force their wives into a feeling of resignation.

Making decisions
Moving on from the question of headship and authority, we shall now look at the way decisions are made within the marriage. Peter was once summoned, alongside other men of

the village, to a meeting where an important issue was to be discussed — the question of a 'settlement plan' with the adjoining village. Peter was always respected for his coolness and wisdom and he and Obi and five other men at the meeting were requested to go up on a certain day to meet a delegation from the adjoining village for an exploratory peace-talk. The peace-meeting would take up the whole day. Obi and four other men gave their consent on the spot. But Peter and the other fellow, who also happened to be a Christian, gave provisional consent, saying they would confirm it when they had reached home.

Whatever reason the other fellow gave for a provisional consent, Peter knew why he had. The selection had been sprung on him. He would go home and talk it over with Esther, for there could well have been an earlier engagement that he had forgotten about, or there might be work in church or some other thing. Esther was to know about this before any decision could be taken.

In the end, Peter did go, but he did not spring it as a surprise on Esther. She knew that he was not going to be in for the whole day and she made her plans accordingly. It may not have happened this way for every Christian in that village but that was the ideal thing. Peter had a right to go but he discussed it with Esther beforehand. Of course, there were times when Peter took a decision on something and informed Esther later, if the situation demanded it. But generally, where he could help it, he always discussed with Esther before he acted.

The traditionalist would argue that a man has a right to do what he wants or to go where he wishes at any time. But Peter was not a traditionalist. He was a Christian. The other Christians in that village tried their best to live out their faith and they found in Peter and Esther a big encouragement. Things have not always been easy for them, but their faith has seen them through.

In Peter and Esther's village there was a time when all children were required to go to clear a piece of land to be used for a celebration which had some pagan connotations. Peter's children fell within the age-range of those required for this task. It had been done year after year, but that year Peter and Esther held council together and after praying decided that their children would not go up for that particular task because it was not glorifying to God. Since becoming Christians they had been trying to face up to issues and always give honour to God. The previous year, they had let their children go up because they did not want to appear uncooperative and so rattle the 'peace' of the village. But now they realized that light and darkness cannot mix.

'Mama,' Peter had asked, 'what do you think about these children going up to clear the "mask-land"?'

Esther kept quiet for some time gazing on the little footstool in front of her. She raised her head, rolled her lovely eyes in her usual manner and said: 'To my own understanding, they should not go. We cannot give our lives to Christ our Saviour and yet have to do with Satan. We teach these children from the Bible every day and we take them to worship every Sunday. We ought not to allow them to join up with the others in this pagan practice.'

'Hmm,' said Peter. 'I have been thinking along those lines too and God has now shown me that my thinking is right. After all, they have nothing to do with the ceremonies; they shall not go up on Saturday. Tell them that.'

The children received the news with joy — they had been saved from a laborious task, it was a Saturday, and there was no school and no church to attend. Yet deep inside their minds was fear — fear of the results of not taking part in this traditional task. For there was a custom that men in masks (representing the living dead) went round all the homes of those not joining in and forcibly collected a fine in cash or in kind. Their mother carefully and clearly explained to them why their father had decided against it and reassured them that the Good Lord was in perfect control. Esther was sure of her facts and could explain it all because thay had discussed it together, even though the decision was finally Peter's. The children found such attitudes reassuring. Their mother's ease over the matter soothed their fears.

Come Saturday and lots of children went up to the task. On Saturday night Peter and Esther's children dreamt about masked figures all around their home. But on Sunday – the usual day for collecting fines – they heard sounds of gongs and music but they saw no masked figures in their home. The children were relieved. Peter had explained his stand over the whole issue. In fact, Peter's stand changed the whole system altogether, setting a precedent. As the years went by, more children from Christian homes began opting out until it became accepted that children from these homes did not join in such tasks.

Peter always fully consulted with Esther on all matters but he gave a final consent to decisions. He knew that was right because of the peace that this attitude produced both inside him and in his wife and household. God had ordained for him to be the head; to guide and lead his family and not to rule them.

In another Christian family, decisions were made in the same way. Tim and Felicia's first boy had passed a qualifying test to get a place in the secondary school. There were two options – the secondary school in the same city they lived and worked in, or another school, which was completely out of town. The city school where he could be a day-student would be a lot cheaper than the school outside the city, whereas he would have to be a boarder in the village school. Most of the other parents were clamouring for the city school because spaces were limited.

One of Tim's colleagues, a traditional city-dweller, asked Tim one afternoon: 'Have you been to confirm your son's acceptance at the school?'

Tim simply replied, 'We have not actually decided yet whether he will be a day-student or a boarder.'

'Who are "we"?'

'Oh! Felicia and I, of course.'

Tim's colleague stared him squarely in the face, shrugged his shoulders and blurted out: 'Do not let the ways of the white man blot out your manhood. Time is short and places are limited. This is no decision for a woman to be involved in.'

'No, thank you,' said Tim, 'ours is different.'

The man picked up his files, took a side-glance at Tim and walked out. He paused at the door, poked his head back into the room and said: 'Anyway, you have just returned.'

He was referring to Tim and Felicia's time in the United States, where they had been at college. Of course that was not the reason. If only his colleague could have known that consultations had been the pattern for Tim and Felicia right from when they got married, long before they went to the United States!

Male cash or shared cash?

It is not only in decision-making that cultural practices and Christian ideals clash. In choosing a wife, most traditional Africans choose somebody who would always rely on them as the sole bread-winner and provider. Even nowadays, when the wife does one type of work or another, the husband will prefer to collect all the money — his and hers — and then decide how it should be spent. Some wives resign themselves to this but a lot have problems with the arrangement. Those who support this system argue that the man is 'ruler' and the traditional bread-winner. Money owned by a woman may make her grow wings. The wings must be clipped in infancy. Where the wife is not working at all, the man finds it easier to act as bread-winner, supplier and boss.

John, mentioned earlier, is a trader. His wife brings his food up to him at the market-shed every afternoon. He has his lunch and tells his wife what he wants to eat for supper that night as well as for lunch the following afternoon. He then gives food-money to his wife, often just enough to buy the necessary things for cooking the meals and no more. 'Leaving excess money in the hands of wives could be dangerous,' they say. 'Never try it.'

It is a very common practice among many African males to give food-money to their wives. This may be daily, weekly or monthly. There is nothing wrong with this practice in itself, if it is done mutually and with full agreement. But often, the wives are not involved in any discussions over this or any other matter relating to money. They say that it would not be in the interest of the man's peace and integrity if his wife should actually know how much money he had.

So the man gives to the woman the amount which he thinks ought to be enough for the upkeep of the home. She can always ask for more, but may or may not be given more. The mere fact of asking for it is what these men want. It helps to establish who is boss. Many housewives in this position go for low-quality food items in order either to make the money go round or to save something for themselves. There have been numerous cases of bitter quarrels and beatings in the home, all because the wife dared to complain or protest over money.

When Tim told his non-Christian workmates that Felicia actually knew how much he took home from work, they thought that was unusual. But when he said that they sat down together to draw up an expense budget, they felt that the 'white man's land', where he had lived with his wife while they were studying, had completely tampered with his thinking and his manhood. One of them concluded that Felicia had discovered the secrets of some 'love charms' which some women are rumoured to use on their husbands, in order to control them. No one had actually seen a proven case of a man living under such a spell, but one of Tim's colleagues was convinced that Tim was a victim of this charm. How else could anyone explain his behaviour? These people found it very difficult to understand that because Tim and Felicia are Christians, they believe in a shared life and in shared responsibility.

For some African Christians, being the family leader does not necessarily mean being the bread-winner. Suppose a man finds his wife bringing home more money than he does. The way the couple have already patterned their life together would determine the degree of peace and stability they would enjoy in those circumstances.

For example, a Christian lady suddenly found herself in a highly paid political appointment. She was well qualified for the job, hard-working and honest. Her take-home pay was high, but though it was much higher than her husband's, it did not disturb or distort the family finances. The couple had always had a joint account in the bank and they had worked out how much was needed each week in running the home; they knew who bought what and why, except the times they gave each other surprise gifts. The children's care and maintenance had also been worked out together. So the extra cash that came from the woman's new salary meant that they, and not she, had more money to spend. I often wonder what would have happened if that woman and her husband were not Christians.

Another young man who also lived in the city started encouraging his wife to do some buying and selling to keep herself busy as well as pulling in some extra cash, since she often complained that her food-money wasn't stretching far enough. She took up the challenge, took some money from her husband and joined a friend in buying all sorts of articles from the big discount merchandise stores, and selling them at open markets.

After about six months, the young man noticed that not only had the quality of the food on his table improved, but also his wife's clothing and grooming. The woman was obviously making money from the venture but was carefully putting her profits in a bank account she had opened, after buying herself beautiful clothes. The man demanded an account of the 'operations' from his wife but received the capital sum he gave to her as a reply. They were not Christians, though they went to church at times. They had never enjoyed a shared life and they had never discussed issues together. The woman started to have a sense of economic freedom and began resisting her husband's authority in many little ways. That marriage has been in trouble ever since.

Some Christians still live unfulfilled family lives because they do not fully comprehend the real meaning of partnership in their marriage. There is a tendency for couples to fall back on their rich African culture and claim that God accepts them as they are. These men claim the Christian principle of the headship of the family because this agrees with their African tradition, but they throw out the responsibility of 'loving their wives so much as to give themselves up for them'. Families such as these often experience problems and it takes sound counselling to bring them back into line.

Many more Christians, however, aim for the ideal. They blend their rich culture into their Christian beliefs, using love as the binding force. Such families experience unmatched happiness and satisfaction and their homes are happy and supportive — both in the cultural sense and in line with what the Bible teaches.

5

Man and Woman

The traditional African has many reasons for taking a wife, but the chief is for the wife to bear and rear his children and so continue his family line. That is why a child-bearing wife usually gets some degree of affection from her husband. If she bears many boys, the favours become pronounced. But if she bears mainly girls, some men start thinking of a second wife while harbouring the first wife. But whether boy- or girl-bearing, the wife still has many different duties.

The traditional, over-burdened wife

The African wife is the cook and the steward for her husband and for the village folk; she and her children are the labour-force for the farm; she knows without being told to join in the work, doing the planting, the weeding, and for certain crops the harvesting. Where she cannot harvest some types of crops she is the main carrier of most of the harvest yields. On top of that she is the one to go to the market, to do the cooking and the washing-up. It is a non-stop cycle. Her only relief is the period of child-birth and the forty or more days following when she is allowed to rest and give some detailed attention to the baby. Some traditions also do not permit her to cook her husband's meals for the brief period of her menstruation.

On top of all that, she is expected to give maximum attention to the children. Not doing any of these things well enough means either laziness or bad home-training — offences which will often influence the kind of 'hand' with which the husband deals with her. When a child is very well-behaved, it is supposed to be a credit to the father who is praised for ruling his family well. But when the child is badly-behaved, the mother bears all the blame. It must be her fault. So she never wins. All these combine to give the African wife a feeling of slavery. She becomes a work-horse with no chance of complaining or escaping. Since it is the accepted traditional practice, there is really no one to turn to. 'It is the lot of women,' you will always hear.

In many cases their plight is not made any easier by the attitudes of mothers-in-law, who still see themselves as the sole overseers of their sons' welfare. In villages where people tend to live on the same compound, mothers-in-law can at times become daylight terrors to their sons' wives. A woman with three or four married sons sees herself as having been given four servants who are not only expected to take care of her sons the way she has always done, but also to take care of her *as well*. This often gives rise to tensions and, at times, clashes between wives and mothers-in-law. Naturally the husband is expected to remain on the same side of the ring as his mother. Most women, therefore, resort to suffering in silence.

It is a different story for the wife's mother. When she visits her son-in-law, she is expected to submerge her personality and help her daughter in seeing that her husband is well looked after and served. Any 'bad behaviour' by her will have serious repercussions on her daughter during her stay and even long after her departure. So, while a woman's mother-in-law enjoys unlimited freedom, her own mother has limited rights and freedom.

That is a picture of the wife's role in a traditional African set-up. How does it differ for a Christian couple like Emmanuel and Comfort?

A Christian husband and wife

Emmanuel and Comfort have been married for ten years now and they have three children — one boy of nine and two pretty girls aged seven and four. The care and upbringing of these children, as well as doing their jobs, keeps them extremely busy and fully occupied. They have their own home in the city, not too far from their parents' homes. Both parents-in-law have now retired from working and live in the village.

Like his father, who is also a Christian, Emmanuel has lovingly led his family. They have had their rough times, their squabbles and their arguments, but they have always come together to the Lord, drawing strength and inspiration from their strong Christian faith. Emmanuel is the head of the family and is a very considerate and understanding man. He works in a big engineering corporation, while Comfort teaches in the primary school. She spends less hours at work than Emmanuel and because the school is walking distance from their home, she often returns hours before Emmanuel does. Comfort has the great responsibility of looking after her husband and their three children, but she is always in high spirits and very exuberant.

Right from the outset, they entered their married life with a big sense of sharing — in a partnership in which Emmanuel was recognized as the senior partner. Like most of his Christian friends, Emmanuel always considers Comfort's feelings at all times — or at least he tries to. He tries to love her as himself, as the Bible teaches. They have always held, and still hold, countless discussions over money, clothing, food and decisions affecting everything. No one partner is in the dark. Both of them always know what is going on in the family.

As an African, Comfort knows what it means to go to the market, do the cooking, do the cleaning, the washing-up, the laundry, and a host of other tasks around the house. It is not easy by any standards, but she accepts the responsibility and throws herself into her chores. It is hard work, and exhausting, but Comfort sees it as a pleasure, rather than a burden. She once told a friend of hers who was listing all her woes about her own house: 'When I remember that I am doing it all for those I deeply love, I derive pleasure from it all.'

Emmanuel knows that this is Comfort's attitude to her

many tasks for the family. And because they do not have any house-helps, unlike some of his colleagues, he tries to share the load with her as much as he can. They also encourage their nine-year-old son to appreciate the joy of helping out in small tasks. Even if they had house-helps, Emmanuel would still have taken some of the work pressure off Comfort because not doing so would be selfish, to say the least. It is obvious that Comfort is not regarded as his work-horse nor his 'house-wife', but his life-partner.

Unlike many other families in the city, they do not have a washing-machine. But instead of leaving Comfort alone to bend over bathfuls of steeped dirty laundry, Emmanuel enjoys sharing the hand-squeezing and wringing of their dirty clothes, which takes up much of their Saturday mornings. Emmanuel is always around the house doing one task or another to help Comfort and she loves it.

When Emmanuel one day told his workmates that what he enjoys doing most in his house is washing-up, some of them nearly had fits. That particular task in the African home is strictly meant for women and children. In fact, one of his workmates got so enraged and agitated over the issue that he took it personally and told Emmanuel he was letting down the whole of manhood. Later he took him out into a secluded area to give him a ticking-off and a 'package' lecture on how to uphold his manhood in his home. When he was done, Emmanuel simply smiled and said: 'Our system works and we are very, very happy together and that is what matters.' His workmate lost hope, lost his temper and walked out. What Emmanuel and Comfort have discovered is that the times they share together in tasks around the house turn out to be very happy times of unity.

Comfort, therefore, does not feel enslaved but has a joyous feeling of freedom. While some other city women get caught up in the women's liberation movement, Comfort always declares that she is not, and never was, in slavery. She feels quite happy with her husband as the head of the family because he is loving, concerned, considerate and kind and never throws his weight about. So, whatever she does in her home, she does voluntarily but dutifully.

Comfort never has any uncomfortable experiences in her relationship with her mother-in-law. There are two main factors responsible for this — the fact that they live apart and, more importantly, the fact that her mother-in-law is a Christian. They have spent a lot of times together, either in their village or in the city when Emmanuel's mother visited. But they have never had any trouble. Somehow, her mother-in-law realizes that the young couple have a right to run their own home the way God gives them the wisdom to. She therefore never pushes Comfort. She simply regards her as her daughter and treats her as such. Emmanuel and Comfort are really blessed in this regard.

The mother-in-law

But not all Christians enjoy their married life in the same way as Emmanuel and Comfort. Even though they have a faith in Christ, they do not sometimes grasp the real Christian essence of marriage and they allow human nature to overcome them. For example, some Christian families have the problem of a sour relationship between mothers-in-law and wives. In nine out of ten cases, the men concerned do not really know the meaning of the biblical teaching on 'leaving' and 'cleaving', stated right at the beginning of the Bible, in the Book of Genesis: 'Therefore a man leaves his father and his mother and cleaves to his wife and they become one flesh.'

This verse is at times most confusing to African Christians. As we saw when we looked at the culture of the people, marriage always involves a woman leaving her parents' home, changing her surname in the process and joining a young man in his own parents' home. So, people often argue, it is the woman who leaves and not the man. What it really means is that the man should also sever the cords of dependence with his family and form a brand-new nucleus, whether he sets up the home in the village or in the city. He too must 'leave' his family. He should love his larger family, but they should not run his home as they ran him when he was young. The African has that concept already — a fellow is not called a 'man' in the real sense of the word till he marries and starts a family — but he fails to stretch it out and apply it God's way. So, those who do not understand this aspect of leaving and cleaving keep having problems between wives and mothers-in-law, because they do not give wives the protection they need.

The African, Christian or non-Christian, always feels a big attachment to his mother. The many cultural songs and sayings about mothers throughout Africa support this. That is the reason why African Christians always find the story of the miracle at Cana in Galilee, where Jesus Christ turned water into wine during a wedding ceremony, easy to understand. Mary spoke to her son, Jesus, about the need for more wine at the feast because the supply had run out. Even though Jesus' reply was, 'Why do you involve me? My time has not yet come,' Mary still went ahead and told the servants to do whatever he told them. The African believes that no son will ever let his mother's plea go by.

For non-Christians there has always been a popular joke in the form of a question and answer to illustrate this: 'If you are travelling on a lonely pathway with your mother and wife and a lion suddenly jumps out of the bush, who do you save first?'

The young men simply shrug their shoulders and reply, 'My mother, of course.'

'Why?'

'I can always find another wife, but I cannot find another mother.'

The old men always nod in approval. 'Wise young man, sensible, good reasoning; hold what you have.' This sort of talk is common among the menfolk in their clubs where women never go.

So, the African Christian who has not really grasped the full meaning and implication of 'leaving and cleaving' tends by his reasoning and actions to go the traditional way. He knows no other way.

Celestina, a young Christian woman, found this a big stumbling block in her marriage. 'I love my husband and I would do anything for him,' she always says, sometimes in tears. 'But one thing I don't understand is why he goes back on our plans each time his mother expresses disapproval or unhappiness. The whole thing started from our wedding arrangements. We had agreed on the venue for the wedding and the reception and we had thought it all through very carefully. But then he changed all that and arranged an alternative venue. In the end it caused a lot of problems for many people. I believe he loves me but I know that he is very close to his mother and any time his mother comes down hard on me, he says nothing. I am confused.' Celestina represents many such Christian women whose husbands need help and counselling and teaching.

In their turn, African mothers-in-law are doing the natural thing for them to do. They find it difficult to let go of their care and deep concern over their sons to some 'young and practically inexperienced lady'. So it is left for the Christian young men to help their mothers to bring their marriages and homes into the right perspective.

Ruth's mother-in-law

Abel is a young, vibrant Christian married to a very charming, capable young Christian lady called Ruth. They live in the city. Abel is very close to his mother, now retired, and he and his wife make frequent visits to the village to see her for weekends or even weeks, whenever they can work it in. He remembers how he was able lovingly to let his mother realize the new position of things.

'It was in our first two months of marriage,' Abel says, 'and we had travelled to the village on the Friday evening to stay with my mother for the weekend. She knew we were coming and had drawn up a comprehensive list of folks we were going to see and had planned how we would achieve this on the

Saturday. She is very proud of me and always enjoys me taking her along to visit the folks she wants us to see. But, this time, when she told me of the plan, I quietly told her that my wife and I had decided to visit her own village on the Saturday because there was something very important she needed to do. At first my mother could not believe what she heard and tried fencing me off by stressing that she had cancelled a lot of things in order to work in this Saturday visit. I had to remind her that she well knew I could never go against her wish if something was not only important, but very, very important. I carefully but gently let her know that I valued my wife's happiness as much as I valued hers and that we could always reschedule her visits, whereas putting off my wife's business could cause irreparable damage. She was not particularly happy, but she gave in.'

According to Abel, they travelled to his wife's village the following day and even though his mother showed some sign of resentment in the way she said bye-bye to his wife, she did get over it. But what put paid to the whole issue was what happened later, as Abel continued his narration.

'Many months later, we were visiting my mother again. This time we had been very busy before our visit, and my wife had borne the brunt of it all. To make matters worse, our little baby was awake most of the night and that kept my wife awake. So, by morning, she was very weak. I asked her to rest in bed while I washed up some bowls and boiled some water for her to feed the baby. To do this, I had to leave the bedroom in the main house, and cross over to the kitchen which was a smaller house detached from the main house − a typical and popular way of building in the slightly advanced modern African village.

'This little journey meant that my mother could easily see me doing the chores. She did! She not only did, but she reacted the way I expected her to react. She sent for me.

' ''Abel,'' she said, ''what is your wife doing inside the house that you should be seen in the kitchen?'' Her voice was a bit icy with a feeling of deep concern and bewilderment. The kind of thing I was doing was supposed to be chores for women and older children. For any wife to ''send'' her husband was a situation that called for the deepest investigation. And my mother was prepared to carry out this investigation.

'I assured her that my wife was sleeping and that I had volunteered to do this so that she could get some more rest, after a hectic day the day before, and a near sleepless night. I further told her that where we live in the city this sort of thing went on all the time. She was already hanging her mouth wide open in an expression of mock shock when I quickly played my trump card and drew a smile from her face.

'I reminded her that she had in the past confided in me that my late father used to do things for her which the normal village man would not dream of doing for his wife. ''I am being my dad's son,'' I concluded.

'She closed her mouth, looked me over, shook her head and smiled. ''You are no good,'' she said.

'Both of us began to laugh and the matter ended there. I gently hit the nail squarely on the head and that clinched it for us. We have always enjoyed our visits and fellowship ever since, because my mother knows we *both* love and care for her, but that I love my wife very, very dearly.'

Hiding from each other

Another problem area is trust and faith in each other. Some Christian couples do not share everything together. Either through ignorance or pressure, they keep a few things to themselves. Once somebody is in the dark about any matter, that person becomes suspicious. And suspicion is the number one tool of the Devil in his attack on Christian homes.

When I walked into the house of a young couple with three young children and a seven-month-old baby, it did not take a special study in human relations to see that the young lady was in an indescribable state of hysteria and confusion. For the first half-hour I could not get any sense out of her. Then, slowly, amidst all the many accusations against her husband, she revealed that she suspected — in fact she was nearly sure of it — that her husband wanted to abandon her and the children, go back to their village and pick up another wife, and start up a new family.

This couple were living in a semi-urban but fast-growing town not far from their village and the wife was convinced that her husband's two trips to the village within the previous six months were in connection with his plan. They both called themselves Christians and I had no reason to doubt them but I knew that they were Christians who had not taken their Bible seriously. I had a serious and deep talk with the young man and discovered that he was only reacting to what he called a 'constant and nagging accusative spirit from my wife'. He had stopped telling her all his plans because most often she found them unwise or foolish and, instead of bringing constructive criticism, mocked and nagged. He had in fact been making the trips back to the village, because he was negotiating to buy a piece of land for them to build a house on. They were not reading the Bible and praying together. They were terribly unhappy.

The advice was straightforward: do not hide things from each other. Criticize, but do not nag. Make meaningful alternative suggestions when ideas don't seem to be right. Above all, read the Bible together and pray together. They have since been on the mend these past years, trying to build up a new relationship based on trust.

Some Christian women also court trouble by pushing the idea of their freedom in Christ and in marriage a bit too far. I remember listening to a young Christian girl who was preparing for her wedding, sharing with two older ladies — married and Christian.

'As soon as the wedding and the honeymoon are over,' she said, 'my husband and I will sit down and share out the housework so each of us knows from the start what is expected.'

She looked for the usual nodding of the head as sign of approval from the ladies, but got none. Instead, they were shaking their heads and roaring with laughter. They tried to advise her to put openness and honesty first and in love learn to cultivate the habit of discussing every issue in order to come to an agreement. If she did this, she would enjoy a life of sharing with her husband. Some women never get this kind of advice or counsel and they go off and push their freedom too far.

The privileged male

Another area where the traditional way contradicts the Christian marriage ideal is the high regard given to men. The traditional man always thinks of himself as being superior in many ways to a woman. His society actually helps to prepare the stage for him in life. For instance, whenever a young woman gives birth to a first baby, people quickly want to find out what the baby is. Happy is the man whose wife's baby is a girl. He is happy because a human being is born. His mates and neighbours and relations congratulate him and give thanks to God that his wife has been led through the rigours of childbirth safely. The women tend to make a big show of it by claiming that they have won the 'victory', and remind the woman that she has got herself a helper in the house. The rejoicing only goes that far.

But if the baby is a boy, the story is quite different. The celebrations often reach a frenzy. Special gifts are bought for the wife because she has produced an heir. Food and drinks flow continuously for days on end — all because a man is born.

Right from this time, all through his infancy and upwards, the African male is encouraged to feel and act out his privileged position. Unwritten village laws are always in his favour. Whereas he is allowed to mimic the monkeys in tree-climbing, it is an abomination for the female — however young — to be seen climbing. He is not allowed to engage in certain types of duties in the house. No wonder then that he grows up to believe that the world belongs to the men and that the women only came along when the men complained to God who made the world that they needed some servants. So, the African man is conditioned to be selfish as far as his relationships with women are concerned. This selfishness shows itself in various ways.

Keeping other women

The first area we shall consider is extra-marital relationships. When the traditional man tells a woman that he wants to marry her, he expects her to feel honoured and happy. It doesn't matter what he is or what he looks like. After all, the Africans say that 'a man is never ugly'. All it means is that whatever a man looks like, he must find some female to marry. Not so with the woman. She is not expected to have a right to choose. Times are fast changing now. The coming of Christianity and the more confusing element of Western influence is bringing about changes.

There was once a story told of a very ugly and seriously deformed African student in one African university who approached a very beautiful girl on the same campus and said: 'My dear girl, being a very choosy fellow, I have looked through all the damsels on this campus and I think you fit the bill for the kind of lass I want to have as my girl. What say you?' The girl responded by dashing off to her room and sobbing her eyes out. It took her close friends many minutes to get the story out of her. She was not a Christian and she could only conclude that for a man like that to make advances to her she must have been cursed.

But that is the traditional man. He feels he has a natural right both to take any woman he likes for his wife *and* to carry on as much as he wants with other women, young or old, in extra-marital relationships. His wife has no right to complain. As one fellow used to brag to his wife: 'You should be happy that I do not bring them home to displace you.' The origin of this attitude, which is common among those who are well-travelled and well-educated, or city-dwellers, can be traced back to the events of generations before. It was and is still a commonly-accepted fact that if a woman has more than one lover in her life at the same time, she is termed useless, a dog, or a prostitute. But when a man has more than one woman in his life at the same time, he is a smart conqueror, an active man and a man of prowess. Just as a big bull services a herd of cattle, so a man's attitude in those days, though frowned upon, was condoned. The practice has persisted till today. And what is the reaction of the womenfolk to it? Resignation and a feeling of 'what can one do?'

A young woman went to her mother to complain that her husband was 'keeping' a lot of women outside and was spending a lot of time in their company. Her mother merely dismissed her complaint. 'Why are you worrying over a situation you cannot change?' she asked. 'Men have always been like that. You have your children to look after and if he gives you enough food-money and buys you clothes and meets your other needs, why worry?' This view is shared by so many non-Christian women and continues to have its effect in society.

It is not that an extra-marital relationship is such a glorious thing and is widely accepted. For anybody with a conscience, there must be a sense of guilt from time to time. But because of the acceptance of polygamy in the society, an extra-marital relationship fails to produce the shock and disgust it otherwise should produce. So it is condoned. At times, people express sympathy for the woman and dislike for the man, but in the end shrug their shoulders as if to say, 'This is a man's world.'

The threat of polygamy

These days, some men take up these relationships as a result of peer-group pressure but claim cultural or traditional immunity. They play their game from an advantaged position. When challenged, they threaten to go the whole way and bring the woman in.

For example, a highly-placed public servant had what everyone thought was a stable and happy marriage. But he started going out with a charming school-teacher who lived in the same semi-urban town. When questioned by his concerned friends, he explained that he needed somebody to 'keep him company' because his wife had a new baby and was completely preoccupied. Of course, before long his wife heard about it and they had a row. His response was to go out and ask for the hand of the lady in marriage from her people. Consent was given because polygamy is an accepted practice. The customary things were done and the lady moved in as an 'authentic' wife and no more as an extra-marital lover. Where before she had trodden carefully, she now trod with uncanny boldness. Now she had equal rights with the first wife. This is why most women neither complain nor make a row over their husband's extra-marital relationships.

Some educated women maintain boyfriends outside their marriage in retaliation. So, deceit mixes with deceit and what you end up with is no marriage at all. The children from such marriages more often than not follow in the footsteps of their parents and help to worsen an already decaying society. All this is the result of the selfishness of the traditional man which he mistakes for his rights and privileges. The bad effects of this can never be measured. Young secretaries, nurses, teachers, students and many other types of women have been lured and deceived and spoilt by Africa's privileged menfolk. At times compensation is paid for these illicit dealings, in cash or in kind, and they most often turn out to be costly to society at large.

Keeping the marriage bed pure

For the committed Christian man, everything is different. In this sort of setting he expresses his Christianity firmly. In God's eye the family is *sacrosanct* and the Christian prayerfully maintains his status before God and man. Christians are often not the most popular people in their work-places or their circles, but they are certainly respected.

One handsome Christian young man lost his rightful privileges in his office because he refused to fall for the seductive approaches of his female boss — a married lady about six years his elder. She kept telling him that her age should not put him off and that he had nothing to lose since any resulting pregnancy could be easily made over to her husband. He is a Christian and so he refused her.

He says it reminded him of a story in the Bible where the wife of a highly-placed Egyptian officer tried to seduce a young, handsome Israelite servant named Joseph. Joseph would only remind her of the absolute trust his master Potiphar placed on him and refused her. But she would not take that for an answer. When at last she cornered Joseph in her room and was about to force herself on him, he left his outer garment in her hands and ran out of the room. She then called in the guards and turned the whole story over against Joseph, 'proving' by her exhibit — Joseph's gown — that her screaming had scared him from raping her. It was her word against Joseph's and Joseph was only a slave in the household. Joseph stood no chance at all, and so was thrown into jail. Because Joseph was innocent and remained honest and trustworthy, God not only rescued him from jail after some time, but placed him high above his former master, next to Pharaoh of Egypt.

This young man never did accept his boss's evil advances and he did not want to create a situation that would give her any advantage. He avoided her in the office and dutifully did his job. When at one point he bluntly refused an invitation from her, she got the message. Her lust was turned into hatred and she began coming down very hard on him, finding fault in most of his work. When at last she wrote a very bad confidential report against him which could have meant either demotion or dismissal, her colleagues disagreed with her. There was a slight stalemate. The young man prayed and waited. Before long, she was given a small rise, transferred to another department and a new boss was brought in. God had fought for that young man in his tender way. The new boss was a man of integrity and the young man's worth was again recognized.

The Christian does not have extra-marital involvements because even though he is an African male, he is an African child of God. And God has strong things to say against extra-marital relationships: 'Marriage should be honoured by all, and the marriage bed kept pure, for God will judge the adulterer and all the sexually immoral.' What applies to the men applies to the Christian women too. But it is true that some African Christians, like Christians in other parts of the world, at different ages and eras, have sometimes been caught out in this very deadly sin. There have been, and will probably continue to be, some 'bad' Christians. A number of them, like King David of the Bible, fall for temptation. Others fall out of ignorance.

African Christians are aware that there are alternatives to Christianity because their tradition and culture are very often steeped in one form of religious rite or another. But in Christ they see the fulfilment of all their yearnings. They are eager to please their Master and Lord. Mistakes are made because they are not taught well, or have not learned what the Bible says on certain issues or situations.

Sometimes, the sin is just a result of the weakness of the will when he or she slips back to the tradition. But when they understand, they do not question. Often, a Christian is caught up in this sin when he or she is still a very young convert and has not really withdrawn from the ways of the world which tradition condones. This does not however rule out an older Christian. After all, Christians do not claim to be perfect; only forgiven.

Thank God, therefore, for the cleansing and sustaining power of the blood of Jesus Christ. Even when Christians are led astray by the evil one and get caught in adultery, the Holy Spirit always convicts them directly or through fellow Christians. Confessions and forgiveness go on and fellowship is restored. The recipe for victory over such temptations is staying close to the Lord through personal devotion and fellowship with other Christians.

Death and mourning customs

The traditional concept of selfishness in the man and the apparent slavery to which women are subjected is also evident in attitudes to death. In so many parts of Africa, a woman whose husband dies often finds herself subjected to so much ceremonial and at times punitive routines that you might wonder whether the poor woman was the disease or the agent of death which killed her husband.

In certain parts of Africa, the woman is not allowed to eat the normal food in the normal way for a lengthy period of time. Her hair is shaven and she is forbidden to venture outside her husband's main living room for a good number of days. Even after these early weeks are past, she wears her mourning garments, usually black, and dresses like that for a complete year. There are many other taboos that she must observe, all in honour of her dead husband. For example, she will not attend any gathering outside her house and will not be allowed even to attend the local market-place for any reason. Any deviation from these or any breaking of the 'laws' means disaster for her. She is accused of insulting the departed spirit of her late husband and harder conditions are likely to be imposed on her.

For the man, the story is different. He mourns for his wife for a few weeks and thereafter has no restrictions on his movements. He wears something to show he is in mourning for his wife and then waits for one year before he remarries if he so desires.

For Christians it is different again. There is respect for the departed but no punitive routines. As the family of God, the church rallies round the bereaved wife to comfort and help. There is usually a memorial service after one month and, in some cases, the restriction of movement for a period of one year is shortened to one to three months, depending on the state of grief of the woman concerned. Here there is a clear example of controlled freedom in Christ. This practice, though begun by Christians, is gaining ground in the society and many are beginning to see the grace and honour in it — grace for the way it is carried out and honour which is given to the woman. These days most working wives who lose their husbands go back to their offices any time after four weeks, depending on the time allowed by their employers.

So, while the traditional practice portrays selfishness even in death, the Christian attitude and practice show deep concern and a good measure of selfless love.

6

Polygamy

No one is sure when the practice of polygamy started but it tends to be very widespread. That is not to say that every African in the past was polygamous, but it used to be a standard practice and still is a standard practice among most unchurched people and some churchgoers.

To the mind of a Westerner the idea of two or three women living in the same house with one husband is preposterous. But an African talking to an English friend put it another way: 'The only difference between our type of polygamy and yours is that you practise "replacing" polygamy because your hearts are not as large as ours.' This remark was meant to amuse, but there is truth in the joke. The African claims that he has a large heart and a 'large barn' and can therefore accommodate as many women as possible, both materially and emotionally. And what this man was trying to tell his English friend was that the average Westerner would have married two or three wives within his lifetime, though he is married to them one after the other, not at the same time.

In whatever way it happens, whether by 'replacing' or by 'joining', polygamy has produced its many stresses and strains down the ages. It goes against the way of life God ordained for men and women in creation — one husband, one wife, for life. We shall look at some of the reasons for polygamy, and some of the arguments used to defend its continued practice. Christianity has a lot to say about polygamy and we shall explore this as well.

Why polygamy?

Why does the traditional African go in for many wives? Many different reasons have been given. Some people actually believe that because it is their tradition, it is therefore part of their culture. But, like all such cultural issues, the practice must have started at some time.

As in all civilizations, the African economy was firstly 'fruit-gathering' and the life-style nomadic, the people moving from place to place. As time went on, they began to settle and to have permanent homesteads. Some continued with fruit-gathering and hunting while others began tilling the ground and harvesting it. When homesteads became settled, each man or family had to defend his territory. Wars between settlements or tribes were quite rampant. All these new ventures and involvements needed able-bodied and strong young men. According to one old African, 'Common sense taught the African that one woman could not produce very many male issues, since no one could ensure every baby born was a boy. He needed more than one wife.'

While it is true that most people had the defence of their own grouping at heart, the real motive for marrying more than one wife was often because of the advantages to the family unit. Wealth was never measured in terms of money or hard currency as we know it today. It was rather measured in farms, barns, animals, property, and land. Land was the real base for generating wealth and that made land very precious. And the land could not be worked without labour. Many African men, therefore, tended to marry two, three, or up to six or more wives because they had a large quantity of land to work.

Many tribes or settlements had chiefs, kings or tribal heads. And very often a man became chief because he excelled over all the others in wealth, strength, or both. These chiefs also had many wives — it is said that some of them had as many as thirty wives. The story is told of a famous African chief who was always being overheard asking young children in his large compound whose child they were. He had so many wives and so many children that he never knew them all.

So, one can understand why the ancient African needed more than one wife. But it is puzzling to find that in modern-day African society, polygamy is still practised. The reasons for this are many. Some simply have not known anything else; it has been practised for a very long time, and because they cannot go far back in time to discover the origin of it among their people, they simply call it tradition. And tradition is never rejected without a very good reason.

Others take more than one wife because it is the common practice among their friends and equals. There was a middle-aged man who suddenly started making plans for marrying a second wife. When questioned by some of his friends, he simply replied, 'My fellow traders have all taken second wives and since they are no better than me economically, why should I be left out?'

Still others go into polygamy because they feel insecure. When a man suddenly realizes that the woman he married is independent and so is not quite as subservient or 'controllable' as he had originally thought, he is advised by his friends to do one 'safe' thing: take another wife. To the Western mind this looks totally unreasonable and suicidal, but to the African it is a 'safe' way out, since he can always manoeuvre the women and keep them worrying over each other.

Many times second or third wives have been given to some well-known people as gifts. It used to be common tradition for a man to 'create' a relationship with a famous or rich fellow by giving his daughter for free to him, hoping to gain from this, by becoming an in-law.

Others take another wife because the first wife does not give birth to as many boys as they desire. In some cases, there are only female children and since the African attaches a lot of importance to the male child, a second wife is at once pro-cured. At times, this backfires.

There was a man who was fairly well educated and had a

well-paid job. He had a wife and six children — all girls. He was encouraged by his friends and family to marry a second wife because he and his wife were both advancing in age. He took up the advice and got a second wife. But the second wife gave birth to only two children — both girls. At this time his second daughter by his first wife, who was not particularly well behaved, ended the way most careless city girls did — she became pregnant. Under normal circumstances her father would have driven her away and made a mock show of disowning her till friends and relatives came round to plead for her. But this was an abnormal circumstance and he did an abnormal thing. He accepted her without too much fuss and took care of her, with the hope that, through her, he would get an heir. She subsequently gave birth to a baby — a bouncing baby girl. At the middle-age of nearly fifty, all the man's hair turned grey. He took to drinking. 'Night,' he said, 'has caught up with me in broad daylight.'

'Needing' another wife

There is a saying in Africa that 'the child who had already determined to run away from home claims that he ran away because he was eyed maliciously'. This is perhaps the only way to describe the reason some Africans give for going into polygamy. They claim to have been pushed into it when all the time they had intended to do it.

I remember sitting down one night opposite one African semi-literate merchant. While 'thumbing' his African dish, he sighed and shook his head and I knew he was going to unburden his mind one way or another. I did the only natural thing.

'What is it?' I asked.

He sighed some more and surveyed the room in which we were sitting, still clutching some of his cold meal in his palm. I followed his gaze as we undertook a silent inspection of that room. It was not particularly tidy. In fact, that was being polite. The room was dirty by all reasonable standards, but had a sense of scruffy order. That was the best his second and very illiterate wife could do.

He had married his first wife some six years before and at that time he felt that being nearly illiterate, though fairly rich as a merchant, he needed a wife more literate than himself, to help bring balance to his home, especially when his business required him to bring home other businessmen. After the first three years, he felt his wife was a bit pushy and feared domination. He thought he could no longer control her and reasoned that the best cure was to marry a completely illiterate woman whom he could control and who would have equal rights with his first wife and, therefore, be able to challenge and curb her.

It didn't quite work out the way he hoped. The first wife claimed seniority and abandoned home-keeping and cooking to the second, while she got preoccupied with outdoor things. The second did not mind because she felt she could cook herself into the man's heart and therefore have more security.

That morning, this merchant had visited the home of another man who had an educated and cultured wife. He had been profoundly impressed by the level of housekeeping and service at table. He finished his silent inspection and rested his eyes on the dining table, on which were stains and traces enough for anyone to figure out what was served for lunch that afternoon. He sighed again and I repeated my question, this time more pointedly.

'What is on your mind?'

The answer followed without any hesitation, as if he was waiting for it. 'I need another wife.'

My eyes nearly popped out of my head as what he said quickly hit home. 'You *need* another wife?'

'Yes,' he nodded. Then he proceeded to tell me how he had nothing to eat all morning except for a cup of tea and a few delicacies he took in his friend's house — the fellow he had visited in the morning. Then he burst out, 'The neatness of the house, the tidy and very clean dining-table and the very polite presentation of the breakfast were more satisfying to me than the breakfast itself. I must get someone like her. Her sister or anyone from her village or family with equal training to take charge of my housekeeping and my cooking. Is it not money?'

'And what about these other wives?'

'Oh, that's simple. I will let them know that their job is to bear me healthy children or . . . I'll find a reason to give them each a furnished room and . . .' His voice tailed away.

I talked the matter over at length with him and finally he saw that he did not actually need another wife. He had for a long time being trying to be 'like the Joneses' — the educated Joneses, that is. His visit to his friend and a fellow businessman that morning blew the top out. As we talked, he began to realize that it was unlikely he would find anyone of the calibre he was aiming at who would agree to marry him as third wife. Then he started being a bit more realistic. When he also realized that he stood a worse chance of being able to control a third wife, judging from his semi-literate first wife, he gave up the idea.

But for whatever reason people in Africa marry many wives, it does not look as if the practice will fade away soon. Only time and change can tell.

The 'benefits' of polygamy

Those who support polygamy claim it has many advantages, but a closer examination produces some baffling and at times disturbing facts. The first and most important thing to note is that whatever is good in polygamy tends to be good only for the *man* who has many wives.

Those who are economically-minded claim that the man is always well-off, since each wife is encouraged to do something in order to see that her section of the family does not suffer unnecessarily. So they claim that the polygamous man's table is never empty. This may be so, but it is not always the case. There used to be a song, often used by those who did not particularly favour polygamy to bring home a point. The song tells a story about a local chieftain who had eleven wives but was constantly a hungry man. The eleven wives were always so busy with their own affairs that each one hoped that the other ten wives had sent up food to the chieftain, so that it did not matter that she had prepared nothing, since there were already ten dishes on the table. As you might have guessed, the chieftain ends up having nothing to eat. This can actually happen. Many African song-stories can often be found in real-life situations.

In support of polygamy, other more depraved minds claim that the polygamous man never lacks bedmates. This might be true for some but things can go wrong. A story is told that during a village get-together, one polygamous man was the centre of ridicule from his mates, because both his wives had just delivered new babies two days apart.

Some people put forward a somewhat silly argument that polygamy in effect reduces the incidence of immorality in society, since the number of single women is reduced. Those who say this do not realize that any man who marries more than one wife at the same time does not really 'love' any of them in the real sense of the word love. There are more cases of adultery and immorality in a polygamous situation than in a one-wife marriage. At any given time a polygamous man's affections tilt only in one direction or even none at all inside his home. There have been extreme situations where the women seek for a more 'satisfying' relationship outside. This might be the reason why certain religions that encourage polygamy also encourage the husbands to lock up the women in 'private quarters'.

Resentment and competition

What are the effects of polygamy on the people involved? They can be very great and far-reaching, often with negative results. Some women who are married to a polygamous man develop a spirit of strife. There is a constant pressure and a sense of destructive competition which is often passed on to the children who grow up to display very selfish and possessive traits. Nothing but a genuine acceptance of Christ can wipe this type of character away. Even after becoming Christians, it takes a long time for such people to overcome these handicaps through the help of the Holy Spirit.

From observation, there are more problems in polygamous homes at the death of the man. In the old days, wives and their children grabbed as much of the man's property as they could, since 'what you get is what you keep'. But in modern times polygamists with even a little education draw up a will and much heartache is caused by the sharing out of the man's property when the will is opened.

While alive, a polygamous man tries to maintain peace among his different wives by using his personality. This is not often achieved, but a patch-up situation is created as things revolve around the man. Remove him, and catastrophe sets in!

One elderly man, who was educated enough to land a job on his country's railways, took a second wife with some arrears he was paid when his promotion was back-dated. He laid down a family law that the young second wife must always respect the first wife and be subject to her authority. He was the sole bread-winner, though the women engaged in petty trading which gave them a little independence and some personal income. The man always gave the family food-money to the older wife who was the overseer. She in turn dispensed with the money according to her judgment, using the younger wife as the entire labour-force in buying and cooking.

During a group discussion on polygamy in an open symposium, this man's daughter was of the very strong opinion that polygamy could be safe and good if properly practised. She outlined the above situation and ended by saying that any man with a strong character can become polygamous any day. In the discussion that followed, she was reminded that things look smoother from her standpoint because she was the daughter to the first wife who had a commanding position. The second wife was 'obedient' at that time, because she had not yet had any male children, and therefore had not 'put down any roots'. The final word to her was that things could not remain the same when either her father died or the male children of the second wife grew up.

In the event, the second situation preceded the first. Several years later, after the birth of her third son, the second wife revolted. At the time her first son was nearly twelve years old. The rough time which resulted perhaps hastened the man's death. Since his death, the problems and squabbles have multiplied.

Scheming and plotting

A man has high expectations of polygamy, but very often those expectations are dashed as he encounters conflict and a failure to make his wives behave in the way he wants them to. Then the situation becomes a nightmare.

Both men and women who are involved in polygamy are often short-sighted and 'wise' only in their own eyes. It is in human nature for a man to believe that he can succeed where so many people have failed. Men who take second, third, or fourth wives trust in their natural ability to contain all those women no matter what. On the other hand, most women who agree to be married to men who already have a wife, or even wives, strongly believe that they will be quite unlike all the others, so totally different in style and tactics that they will be able to turn the man's heart to themselves, and only themselves, for ever. But that is not the case at all. No wonder there is this saying in Africa: 'It doesn't take too long for a new and shiny cooking pot to see why the older cooking pots lose their shine.'

So the two parties scheme and plan, and in most cases the plans clash with very painful results. As the man plans against his wives, so the wives scheme against the man and against each other. The reason for all the planning and scheming is that the multiple co-wives almost immediately discover that life in a polygamous situation is one of ever-shifting emotions and misplaced loyalty. In many cases the man succeeds in outwitting or outscheming his wives, but sometimes the women combine their plans. This is an ever-present danger for the man.

Adikwu came from a tradition that holds that for as long as a woman is breast-feeding her baby, there should be no sexual meeting with her husband. So, Adikwu had gone out to marry a second wife because his first wife, for reasons best known to her, continued breast-feeding her baby for over two-and-a-half years. For the next few years things worked out for Adikwu, but meanwhile the wives realized that his real reason for getting two wives was merely physical and selfish. There was always a sense of rejection for the wife who was not warming his sleeping-place.

The wives could do nothing about it until by a stroke of 'ill luck' both of them became pregnant at the same period. It was when they both delivered within two days of each other that he became the village joke. When the two women realized their strong position, they decided to make the most of it. Adikwu was faced with either taking better care of them or going to marry a third wife. Conditions for him at that time were not favourable for taking a third wife. He could not afford it. . .

Such situations may be rare but they do occur, and whenever they do the man always has a little taste of his own poison. On the other hand, it is more common and easier for the man to cause untold heartaches to some of the women he 'collects'. The common saying is that a polygamous man retains his peace and sanity as long as he keeps the women going at each other's throats. The man then plays the peace-maker and rides free.

There are many ways of making sure that the wives are always against one another, but the simplest is to conspicuously shift affections, even if it has to be faked. And, on top of that, the man behaves as if he has no idea that things are not all right. Deep within the culture is the advice: 'Always give them things to share; never share for them. If they are two, give them three tubers. If they are three, give them five. *And* make sure that it is something that can't be easily halved.'

Okonkwo's dilemma

Oftentimes, however, the women's quarrels affect the peace of the man, as is only to be expected. Okonkwo was a farmer and always loved coming home after a hard day's work, following a visit to the market-square where he had 'sat astride' pots of palm-wine with his fellow men – an equivalent of going to the local pub with friends for an evening's drink. He was rather successful and showed it by taking a village title, as well as a second wife.

This second wife happened to acquire the rather rare gift of talkativeness and, having been advised by her mother, entered into strife straight away with the first wife in order to 'get her ground' early. The first wife would have preferred to settle most of these issues by physical combat. Not so the second wife, who relied on her non-stop tongue-lashings that cut deeper and sharper than a knife-edge. Though she worked hard, her provocative taunts and unwarranted squabbles made her lose Okonkwo's favour. The only mistake he made was to side with his first wife and to scold the young verbal warrior. This spurred his first wife into haltingly hurling back some of the abuse.

Perhaps it was that or Okonkwo's action, no one knew, but what happened next took both of them by storm. This human talking-machine spurted out such unprintable abuse at such a speed and high pitch, that an old car engine couldn't have done better. Both Okonkwo and his first wife darted away from the scene as if pursued by a whirlwind. The first wife ran into her hut while Okonkwo disappeared behind the central beams that held his house in place. Of course, there was no place to hide away from the hail of words outside.

The poor man quickly went off to the village market-place where he could at least listen to his fellow men and drink his palm-wine in peace. The pattern was thus created. He did not have to make any further effort at making his two wives go against each other. He himself was caught by the web he had spun for them. The incessant quarrels were driving him crazy. He began to escape from his home. Okonkwo had created a living hell for himself and he had no one but himself to blame.

Christians and polygamy

We have looked at many aspects of polygamy; we have investigated the claims of its supporters and looked at its effects on both men and women. But what does the African Christian think of polygamy? There can only be one answer to that question — *God forbid!* Many African Christians have had brush-ups with polygamy, if not with their immediate family setting, then with their grandfather's family. So they are often in a good position to see the very bad effects of polygamy.

Let us go back in history to the time when the missionaries first came to Africa. They found the whole question of polygamy extremely difficult, and had very hard decisions to make. When a man who had two or more wives became a Christian, he was advised to put away all the wives but the one he wished to 'wed' with. That was simple, but it was an injurious way out of the problem. It was simple because the matter was straightforward and, once complied with, led to baptism and wedding.

For the missionary coming from a Western culture which did not have polygamy, the matter was simple and straightforward indeed. There was no other reasonable alternative. They congratulated themselves on a job well done, but no one stopped to ask what became of those women who were sent away. There was no sort of settlement for their maintenance. Many of them went home to their family and just had children for any man that came along and so earned their keep. This created its own moral problems, and made those who had been so shabbily treated resistant to the message of the Christian gospel.

One cannot really blame the missionaries because they were

grappling with a dilemma — the church of Jesus Christ needed to be based on sound biblical principles of purity; polygamy would be a compromise. Therefore they took a difficult decision in the face of a difficult problem. I have often wondered why the Apostle Paul in the Bible kept quiet on the issue of polygamy. From all indications, the problem must have existed, for he commanded that any man desiring office as an elder or deacon should be the husband of only one wife.

The situation that the missionaries left us was reviewed when the church in Africa grew and nominalism (people being Christians in name only) crept into the church. Stringent regulations like exclusion from Holy Communion became relaxed in some areas, and others began to question the fairness of the whole Christian practice of sending away the married women. Some had been married for many years and had children and had put down their roots very strongly.

It is sad to note that one group of African 'converts' of a particular denomination became so enraged over the whole issue of polygamy that they broke away and formed their own indigenous church. Polygamy was entrenched as one of the practices of their church and was not to be tampered with for any reason. If anything, it was argued, the church should uphold such a 'noble' African tradition which is one of the distinctive features of African marriage.

The arguments normally used to support their case are drawn from the lives of early personalities of the Bible who were all polygamous. Abraham and Jacob found favour with God, and even King David, that famous King of Israel who was also polygamous, was described as 'a man after God's heart'. They also argue that God's command in Genesis, the first book of the Bible, is that we should 'increase and multiply and fill the earth'. We cannot easily do this, they claim, if every man marries one wife. Again, statistics show that there are a lot more women than men, the argument continues. Marrying more than one wife will give the women who otherwise cannot find a husband a chance to get married. So they argue that they are actually helping society to solve the problem of spinsterhood, still thought of as a disaster in African society.

But against all these 'noble' ideas and arguments, they fail to recognize the fact that none of those polygamous families in the Bible whom they use to support their point of view, ever had peace in the real terms of family peace. They were all riddled with strife and quarrels. God used them to warn us. But such is this perversion that no one in this church can be ordained as a minister unless he has at least two wives.

The attitude of committed African Christians towards all this is not one of condemnation but of prayer — prayer for such people that God may help them to see that the evil effects and disadvantages of polygamy far outweigh any good that it is claimed to bring to society.

Solving the problems

In tackling the problems of polygamy, Christians start with the Bible. There is no doubt that God intended marriage to be a union between two people only. 'A man,' the Bible says, 'should leave his father and mother and cleave to his wife and they shall be one flesh.' It is for the same reason that Jesus warned his hearers with these words: 'Therefore, what God has joined together, let no man put asunder.' To have a second wife intruding on that union would be breaking the bond between a husband and wife. So there is no question about whether the African Christian, or any Christian, should take a second wife. It is wrong; it is unbiblical; it is sinful. Where the church is firm on this, even nominal Christians accept that polygamy is wrong.

There is a problem, however, when an unchurched man, or even a nominal Christian, accepts Jesus Christ as his personal Saviour and begins to live life committed to following him. What does he do with the extra wives he has 'collected' during his time of ignorance? Many committed Christians in Africa today believe that any polygamist who becomes a committed

Christian should be left to be led by the Lord to examine his own conscience, trusting in the Holy Spirit to deal with the individual in his own situation. After much prayer and deliberation in the presence of the Lord, what the Lord convinces him to do should be his final decision on the matter.

A man is no longer encouraged to send anyone away. Attempts to make laws have been found inadequate. Some said that the man should simply house and feed and generally maintain all the wives without any further sexual intimacy with them, except with the first one who is his lawful wife. This is easier said than done in a situation where the man has lived with the women as his wives. Having a constant temptation at his doorstep, it would not be surprising if he failed the test.

Other men have explained the changed situation to their wives and given them the option to leave while assuring them of their continued maintenance. Some wives take up the option and leave, but if they do not the problem remains. The matter, however, is often made easier if the women concerned become Christians.

Aduke is the third wife of a rich man. She became a Christian and, according to her, 'God convicted me over the idea that I was living in sin.' She was doing some trading and so determined that if God granted her the means, she would leave her husband and stay on her own with the children she already had. While she was waiting to move out, she left her husband in no doubt as to her new-found faith. This brought some strain into the relationship which made it easy for her to pull out of her sexual commitments to her husband. In fact, it would be more correct to say that her husband became disenchanted with her and stopped seeing her. As the Lord blessed her, she was able to afford a small rented accommodation and moved away with her children.

Is that the solution to the problem? It does not pay to be dogmatic at this point. One thing is certain: the Lord will always find a solution to the problem for the Adukes of the Christian fold once they are willing to be obedient to him. He will always give guidance for each situation. Since all situations cannot be the same, legislation may cause more problems than it can solve.

Facing up to family pressures

Nevertheless, there are pressures. The African Christian is a child of God and, therefore, belongs to the family of God. But the African, humanly speaking, is an African. Very often he or she may face dilemmas and undergo a lot of pressures from the family if they are not Christians at all or have a very shallow faith.

One of the commonest reasons for the family and friends of an African Christian to pressure him to marry a second wife is the issue of childlessness. Most Africans believe that the main reason for marriage is for children to be produced to continue the family line.

Charlie, a young Christian man, loathed travelling home to his village from the city because his family was dead-set on making him take a second wife. He and his wife had been married for five years and had not had any children. Charles loved the Lord and he loved his wife and would not willingly do anything to displease either of them. So he rejected and resisted the family pressure. He strongly believed that if the Good Lord wanted to bless his marriage with a child, he would do it, so he encouraged his wife to have a strong faith over the issue and not to worry. The 'tug-of-war' continued and people began ruling him out as crazy. But ten years after their marriage, the Lord blessed them with a baby boy. Charlie was justified in his belief, the Lord's name was glorified and Charlie had an opportunity to share his faith with his family.

Other reasons a family may have for persuading a man to take a second wife could be the fact that only girls were born or that the wife is ill and therefore cannot deliver babies. These pressures are often not light, but the child of God in Africa knows that with God nothing is impossible.

7

Divorce

In any situation, when the centre ceases to hold together, things begin to fall apart. In marriage, it is no different. Tensions mount and tempers become shorter. Trust disappears and affection turns into indifference or even hate. Joy and happiness are replaced by agony and pain. The inevitable happens — complete breakdown and separation. That which has been joined together is then torn apart. Divorce in a marriage is rather like death, except that the people concerned still remain alive. The death of a marriage union produces its own type of pain and remorse.

This concept of divorce is looked at differently in different parts of the world. To the Westerner in a Western culture, divorce is very business-like and has its own rules and regulations to protect both the male and female partners. To the African and some other cultures, there is a one-sided slant. Where a marriage is concluded by native law and custom, the ending of that marriage takes the same pattern — more the 'putting away' of a wife rather than divorce. It is only now that laws concerning marriage breakdowns and dissolutions in Africa are being brought in which compare with what takes place in other civilized parts of the world.

The family factor
The divorce rate in Western society is very high — said to be as high as one in three. By comparison, the divorce rate in Africa is much lower, mainly because of the pattern of marriage and the place of the single family unit within the larger family. As we saw earlier, a woman gets married to her

husband but also she marries into his family. That is why there is often a huge family presence at all stages of the marriage arrangement. Because of the 'togetherness' of the larger family, any man or woman has a number of older folks to talk to if there are problems within their marriage. Again, because of closeness in the larger family, it is very easy to notice when a marriage relationship begins to turn sour. Questions are at once asked and, at times, there are direct interventions by members of the family or friends.

I remember one incident that clearly illustrates this. There was a fellow whose wife suddenly developed an obsession for looking trim. She had complained to her husband that he was not buying her lovely dresses from the shops, but he had explained that it was very difficult to find large and extra-large sizes to fit her. So she had decided to slim down. It was then that the African sense of 'concern for my brother' showed up. For a plump African married woman suddenly to start looking thin must either mean that business was not going on well or that trouble with her husband was keeping her awake at nights. After all, there is a saying that 'frogs do not run in the afternoon for nothing'. The first was ruled out because everyone knew that his trade was going on well. So they concluded that there was trouble between her and her husband and something must be done about it.

When the African makes your affair his business, it is not considered an intrusion into your privacy, but it is genuine concern and must be treated as such. When the wife was telling me about this incident, she said that up to three different women asked her why she was suffering in silence and suggested that she should talk to the elders about her problems with her husband. Her husband also had other men come to him to find out what the matter was.

'Your wife is telling the whole story by her looks,' they told him. 'Confide in us; we can always help.'

The poor lady said they kept assuring everyone that nothing was wrong, but no one was convinced. The tell-tale signs were too obvious. 'I blame it,' she moaned, 'on my decision to lose weight.'

This is the kind of support that the African family gives, to ensure a continuous and uninterrupted married life. But this does not mean that marriages do not break down or that women are not 'put away' or sent home.

Do you meet my expectations?

There are many reasons why African marriages break down, leading either to the woman being sent home or divorce. Except in cases of illness or disease, all the reasons stem from one thing — expectations.

We saw earlier that in the strict African sense, marriages are entered into through families. The marriage partners may have met before getting their families involved, or may have only been introduced through their families. In either case, the couple may not have had enough time to know each other well enough to make a personal decision. Very often the couple get married on family reputations and expectations. Before they were married, each partner had a set of standards which they expected from the other. For women, it is often a strong and energetic man, able to provide and protect, and well able to stand his ground among his peers. And for men, a wife is somebody humble, home-bound and always ready to answer at his beck and call; well versed in the art of cooking and with good 'stewardess manners'. She must not be someone who talks back or who talks much; but rather someone to respond to instructions. Above all, she must be chaste and faithful.

In so many cases the woman is expected to fit the man's bill down to the last detail, but she should be grateful herself if only one, or indeed any, of her own expectations are merely touched on, let alone fulfilled. She is expected to be the grateful partner because she is the one being married. This way of thinking is what often leads to breakdowns in African marriages. It is a problem of background and tradition. Since the man marries a woman because he needs a servant, a worker and a bearer of children, it stands to reason (at least, to his) that performance below his expectations calls for a review and, at times, action.

The choice of a marriage partner is often regarded as the purchase of equipment. If the equipment does not perform very well, but is manageable, it can be retained and a new one acquired to increase the productivity of the old one. Where it is too bad and cannot be managed, it is returned to the seller. This idea sounds preposterous and debasing to the womenfolk, but that is what it is for the traditional African. Marriages have therefore been broken or dissolved (though rarely) because the woman has not lived up to the expectations of the man. During some of the ceremonies marking the completion of the marriage contract one can overhear the womenfolk admonishing the new wife in song: 'When you cook well for him you have peace; but when your cooking turns bad, the pot "breaks on your head".' In a way this shows the acceptance of their lot by the womenfolk − a situation created and conditioned by years of tradition and practice.

Mending damaged marriages

Having said all this, it must be said that for a marriage to reach divorce, it must be proved beyond any reasonable doubt that the marriage cannot be mended or patched up. Just as it takes all that time to acquire a wife, it takes equally as long, if not longer, to get rid of the marriage. There are often numerous consultations. Families are brought together on both sides. The problems are looked into and attempts are made at solving them. Once a problem in a marriage is spotted or a complaint is lodged, the issue is immediately taken up. Depending on the type of problem, by the time the matter goes through the first, second, third or more stages of consultation, it is usually resolved.

Oraefo, a middle-aged farmer, was hosting a little party for his large family and a few friends in the village. He was celebrating the return of his wife from her parents' home where she had been for the past many months. Earlier in the year there had been problems and he had sent messages through a neutral individual in the village to his in-laws, complaining of his wife's misbehaviour. This messenger had no blood relationship with either Oraefo or his in-laws, so that he could never be accused of taking sides.

Each time the messenger's communications had sounded more desperate and threatening. But the wife's parents did nothing, possibly because they underestimated the size of the problem. From their point of view, they did not consider the complaints demanded a major intervention. They decided they would send for their daughter at a convenient time and caution her. But meanwhile, Oraefo's patience snapped. He gave the wife a thorough beating and sent her packing to her parents. When her parents saw her, they knew she wasn't coming for an ordinary visit. She had been sent away from her matrimonial home. Then they were forced to send for their son-in-law. . . Now Oraefo was celebrating his wife's return, but it had taken four meetings by both families within the space of six months.

It is not always the husbands who initiate talks over marriage problems. There are obvious instances of maltreatment by the husband. In this case the wife often sends messages home to make a report to her mother or, in her absence, a prominent female member of her family. The matter gets passed up to the father or the menfolk. When it is a proven case of wickedness or even unreasonableness by the man, the woman's family sends a note of warning or threat – of taking the woman away from the man. It is at this point, very often, that the man initiates consultations with the woman's family, and the conflict is resolved or patched up.

This type of situation is more common among women who come from very influential or well-to-do families. Such actions would always remind the man's family that the woman has a strong family backing and therefore should be handled with care. There is a popular saying: 'The person who has people has a better standing than the one who has wealth.' In these circumstances it is the wife's expectations that are not reached and she complains.

For the traditional African, therefore , marriage is not based on 'for better, for worse . . . till death do us part', as it is for Christians. It is 'for as long as you live according to my expectations and for as long as you perform your functions adequately'. The men unfortunately have an advantaged position in this arrangement, though there is a strong fight by the literate womenfolk in modern African society to tip the balance and make it fair. It has not been an easy task.

'Sending home' and going home

Sometimes, starting to talk over the marriage problem takes quite a simple form. When Mambo sent for his parents-in-law to visit him and their daughter in the city, little did they realize that they were in for a surprise. They had both been excited at the prospect of going to stay for two days with their son-in-law. It was on the second night, after their supper, that Mambo sat down with them and his wife and laid before them his complaints and his intention to send their daughter home if she did not mend her ways. They were shocked but happy that he had not made the whole issue a public affair. When he went to work the following day, they had a good heart-to-heart talk with their daughter. At least now she knew that they knew. They could help her and the matter was nipped in the bud.

In some traditions, the 'sending home' is more dramatic. I was told that when a 'problem wife' is asked by her husband to accompany him on a visit to her people she may not in fact know that she is being sent home. The man invites some other relations to go along with him and his wife. From all indications, the visit looks normal. They carry different types of gifts and some pots of palm-wine. It is only the type of pot carried by the wife that tells the whole story for 'those who understand'. She is given a pot of palm-wine to carry on her head alongside other women, but on nearing her father's house, a bunch of green leaves of a particular tree is placed over the mouth of the pot. One look at the pot, and the older members of the family know the nature of their 'visit'. The visitors are well received and there is even eating and drinking and slight merriment. When it is time to depart, the wife is asked by her family to stay back for some more time as her husband and his people return to their own home. Meetings and talks are held to resolve whatever problems there are in the following weeks. That, we are told, is the idea behind the cynical remark from a husband to his wife after some disagreement or quarrel: 'We will soon visit your people.'

As for the women who are maltreated, the easiest way to find help or to ask for the nullification of the marriage is for her to run back home to her people. If the husband is keen on getting her back, he makes the difficult trip to his parents-in-law to 'look for his wife'. Other times her parents send for her. As soon as she arrives, a message is despatched to her husband clearly stating that he has to come and get her.

Quarrelling, violence, bad cooking . . .

Reasons for sending home a wife or for a wife to run home for herself are many. Some are serious while others are mere trifles, depending on the person concerned. Remember clearly that the bond is not 'till death do us part', but 'as long as you fit my bill'.

The most common reasons given by men for sending their wives away, or considering doing so, are bad behaviour and a spirit of contention. This often makes the woman very disagreeable to her husband. The spirit of contention shows in the quarrelsome attitude of the woman both to her husband and the neighbours. This destroys the peace the man desires at home. His time is taken up in dealing with particular issues, or making peace between her and her neighbours. A man ceases to 'drink water and keep his cup', as they say.

It follows naturally that a quarrelsome and badly behaved woman cannot at the same time be humble and respectful —

two qualities which are cherished by African males. Other reasons are bad cooking and apparent lack of orderliness in housekeeping. The traditional African male believes that the woman by nature should know how to keep house and should be able to pick up how to cook from her mother. A man may only be able to make allowances up to a certain point before thinking about nullifying the union and ending the marriage. There are other flimsy reasons like bad temperament and bad sleeping habits. They may seem flimsy to us, but the man in question would argue that 'he who wears the shoe knows where and how it hurts'.

As for the womenfolk, the most serious reason is maltreatment — either because the woman's needs, as well as those of the children, if any, are not adequately met, or because of actual physical violence. Many ordinary African women accept that they can always be beaten by their husbands when they 'offend'. However, when this beating becomes violent and arises from animosity and hatred, the woman often runs away to her home or a relation. Some women find they cannot stand a miserly or a very selfish man. The words 'very selfish' are chosen because all women expect a measure of selfishness from their husbands, but when it becomes a constant factor, it creates problems.

Ogbeya's problem was that his wife could not cook. This is a real problem to the African wife. Unlike Western women, she has no access to any sort of cookery book to help her. There were not any then; even now, the few there are would not be very helpful if she had missed the opportunity to learn how to cook when she was growing up at home with her mother. Ogbeya's wife was in real trouble.

Ogbeya was a craftsman and his job always took him long hours of concentration and sweat. He worked with wood. He had to have at least one good meal a day. He was not asking for 'concoctions', which was exactly what his wife was dishing out for him every day. What made matters worse was that Ogbeya brought in a customer and a meal was offered him in true African fashion, since it was a meal-time. The food was over-salted and inedible. The visitor was very polite but could not eat much of it. He stopped eating as politely as he had started. Because he was a craftsman, Ogbeya was a man who never missed details, however small. But that was not the first, second or third time that this had happened. Ogbeya could not bear the disgrace any longer. He sent her home.

Many weeks passed, but Ogbeya did not send for his wife. His parents-in-law sent to find out why he had not done anything. He did not wish to have any meetings or talks over the issue. He was finished with it. Nothing could change his mind or the situation since it was already too late for the woman to start cookery lessons all over again. That ended the matter. The subsequent meetings held by both families were just to formalize the break.

Reasons not to get divorced

Of all the numerous cases of quarrels, complaints and sendings away, only a few end up in actual divorce or separation. Within the village setting, no African wants to see his marriage break up. This is because consideration is often given for the reputation of the larger family. The more prominent the family, the more difficult it is for them to accept a total break-up as this will tarnish the family image. If it is the man's family that is reputable, they may be branded 'that family that does not know how to take care of wives', and so other reputable families will not want to give their daughters in marriage to them. If it is the woman's family, they may be branded 'that family whose daughters make bad wives' and this will affect the chances of the yet unmarried girls in the family. Rather than a total break, the families will encourage a patch-up to save the family name.

It is true that some men are quick in sending their wives away or that some women are quick in running home to their families, but all that tells us is that the one who takes the initiative is crying out for help. There are no professional marriage counsellors of any sort, so it is up to the larger families of both the man and the woman to mediate and settle the disputes and help make the necessary repairs to the relationship. Families, at their best, are always prepared to exhaust all possible options in their search for peace. They are prepared to patiently and impartially look into the problems till a compromise is reached. It is only when there is no other way to mend it that the marriage is allowed to fall apart.

Another reason why marriages are not annulled very easily is because of polygamy. When a woman is very quarrelsome or is so bad that life becomes unbearable for the man (that is the story from the man's point of view), he can either have the whole situation referred to his in-laws or he goes ahead and takes a second wife. The second, it is always claimed, becomes a balance for the first, and the man is let off the hook. If, however, the first proves doubly unbearable, she is disowned by the husband and sent back to her people.

Nobody wants a bad relationship with his in-laws where it can be helped. After all, at the time of acquiring a wife, enough time and opportunity are given for any possible withdrawal from the whole thing. Having gone through all that rigour, people do not want to be accused of not being careful and observant before committing themselves. The defence by the would-be accused is in the popular African saying that 'women arrive at their husbands' homes with many hidden parcels which they open in stages', so it is never possible to know what a woman is like until you start living with her. In modern times, they say it is like ordering a commodity from a catalogue. What you see may not necessarily be what you get. Needless to say, the feeling is mutual. Time and time again you hear a distraught wife say: 'If I knew then what I know now; if I knew this is how he would turn out to be, I would never have married him.'

The difference children make
For the women who feel they are getting a raw deal from their

husbands, certain other factors affect their attitude to the problem. Nembe always got beaten up by her husband who came home drunk most days. She left him for her father's house on two occasions. Each time the man had come and made promises and pledges and she had followed him home, only to be subjected to the same treatment. There had been a long spell of peace, though, after she came back the first time. But then he started beating her again. That was why she ran away the second time. Again the man had come with his people and taken her back. He is still beating her now and is still getting drunk, but she has decided not to go any more. Her children are growing up and they need her. When they become teenagers, he will not dare touch her again.

Eunice, an illiterate woman with six grown-up children, now in her early sixties, told of her experience when she was younger. Her husband was always fond of beating her up because, according to him, it was the only thing that stopped her mouth. Eunice actually has one of those 'mouths' and if at this age the 'sting' is still in her mouth one wonders what it used to be like in her younger days. Having drawn attention to her problem by going home, she decided to stop going or complaining after the birth of her third child. Her maltreatment continued but she bore it through to her sixth pregnancy. It was three years after this that the issue resolved itself.

By this time, the older children were all teenagers and they were all in one morning when another row developed. Her only defence was her mouth and no sooner had she started to lash out at him than the husband did what he had perfected. This morning, though, the story was different. As soon as he pounced on her to 'stop her mouth', the two big boys and their sister came round to stop him. The fourth and fifth, a boy and girl respectively, also came with 'little' weapons — a stick and their teeth. The girl landed the stick on his waist while the boy jumped and dug into his dad's neck with his teeth. The older ones challenged him to a boxing contest, landing the blows indiscriminately all over him.

The encounter was swift but effective. He backed off in utter bewilderment and shock as Eunice kept grinning and taunting: 'I have people,' she kept saying, 'I am no more alone and my day has just broken.' That was the last time she remembered her husband ever attempting to beat her up. Their squabbles continued but in her children she knew she had roots. They are still living together, both of them having put those difficult years behind them.

Eunice's experience is not an isolated one. Many other grown-up children have been known to curb their father's physical violence on their mother by giving him a dose of his own medicine. The effect is always the same. Where there are no children, the matter can be different. Often, the woman who has 'nothing to lose' — who has no children, in other words — decides to save herself the physical pain and quietly leaves for her own home, where she lives for the rest of her life in peace.

However, in extreme circumstances, a woman gets to the point where she cannot bear the violence any longer and so leaves her children and goes home to her people for good. Since many people do not go to court to get a divorce, the custody of the children is not contested at all. They belong to the man. In African society, it is an accepted fact that children belong to the man. So when a marriage breaks down and the woman leaves, she gives up her rights to the children. That is why most women would stay no matter what happens to them. They cannot bear the thought of another woman bringing up their children for them and possibly harming them in the process. The situation is, however, different with educated city-dwellers, as we shall soon see.

Traditionally, a man sees divorce (sending the wife away, that is) as the only way out if the woman becomes insane, has a bad disease or is involved in adultery or other forms of immorality. Not so the women. A woman whose husband is involved in adultery does not think of divorce. She simply accepts the situation. And where there are children, a woman is always reluctant to go.

Changing patterns of divorce

So, to the traditional illiterate or semi-literate African family in the village or urban towns, divorce is seen as something possible but not always probable; as an unfortunate inevitable rather than a ready alternative to a broken-down marriage relationship. The only areas where the divorce rate seems to be slightly high are those areas where the low bride-price, coupled with a shorter process of acquiring a wife, makes it easy for a man or woman to ditch a partner and look for another. But such cultural areas are comparatively few and even then the rate of divorce is not very high.

The newly-emerging educated city-dweller is different, however. The divorce rate among this class of people has been on the increase since the last decade. Education brings about a realization of the rights and privileges of an individual in society. I know of a young woman who bought and read books concerning her legal rights as a wife. Armed with this information, she made life unbearable for the man, always quoting the law to show him that he could do very little about it since she was within her rights. This may be an extreme situation, but there is no doubt that this kind of knowledge is becoming counter-productive. People now go to court for both serious and flimsy reasons and, because they always have the common law as a tool, obtain their 'freedom' through divorce.

So it seems that common law replaces the wise old men from the families who sit together for many days, or even weeks, to see that marriages are not allowed to disintegrate. The only deterrent to some of these newly-emerging educated people is the legal requirement that money be paid to women who are divorced by their husbands. Rather than pay this alimony, the affected men simply slump into polygamy and avoid going through with a divorce. Whether this new awareness and practice is a good or bad thing is an issue for continued debate.

But most Africans agree that though there is no alimony in native divorce the rate is still very low. The determination to carry on in the face of problems but with the help of the larger family is something which the African will always be proud of.

Christians and divorce?

We have looked at attitudes to divorce in the context of traditional African marriage, and in the new city-dwellers of Africa. But what is the Christian view on this? With the African Christian, the possibility of divorce is not even introduced when discussing marriage problems. In a tradition in which divorce is only nominally practised, the African Christian sees the need to follow the Bible's teaching to show that he or she has something special, something different.

A committed Christian had a wife who became very ill and who then had a mental breakdown from which she has not recovered. Though she is now in a mental institution, her husband makes it a point of duty to visit her every Sunday afternoon. Relations, friends and well-wishers have been pressurizing him into taking another wife, but he always has one answer: 'For better, for worse; in sickness or in health . . . till death do us part. That is the vow I made before God. My wife is not dead; she is only ill. If God wants me to marry again, she will die.' The people who hear this are baffled, but the man is highly respected.

Back to biblical teaching

But is there any allowance for divorce in Christian teaching? We read in Matthew's Gospel, chapter nineteen, that Jesus made a categorical statement on marriage: 'Have you not read that he who made them from the beginning made them male and female, and said, "For this reason a man shall leave his father and mother and be joined to his wife, and the two shall become one flesh"? So they are no longer two but one flesh. What therefore God has joined together, let not man put asunder.'

The saying is hard to take nowadays. It was hard for them as well in those days because they argued back: 'Why then did Moses command one to give a certificate of divorce, and to put her away?' The answer was easy and Jesus supplied it: 'For your hardness of heart Moses allowed you to divorce your wives, but from the beginning it was not so.'

In those days people found reasons to put their wives away and they asked for authority. Moses gave it. But Jesus said that was not what God intended. These days people are putting away their wives, or want to put away their wives or even husbands, and they are looking for authority. Common law is supplying that authority, and in different nations we can see examples of immorality, of ignorance of God's laws. Because God's standards seem very difficult, people seek easy options and all sorts of excuses to avoid facing up to them.

When African Christians meet Christians from a Western culture and hear about divorce based on a complete breakdown of the marriage, they are confused. There are three reasons for this. First, they cannot see any biblical justification for divorce on such grounds. As they see it, when a relationship breaks down, it is because the people concerned are unwilling to make the necessary sacrifices to restore it. A breakdown can be remedied if the two people are willing to give God a chance to change their situation. Often the problem is that such Christians believe that divorce is an option and so they do not make every effort to stop their relationship declining. If as Christians we truly believe that we belong to and serve an all-powerful, living God, then it will not be too difficult to accept that he can mend a broken marriage relationship. And believing that, give him every chance to do it. Second, African Christians are confused because even among non-Christians in the traditional African culture, the families rally round and try to sort things out between the two people.

But the third point is even more confusing. Jesus Christ said point-blank in the Bible that there should be no divorce except for adultery and immorality: 'I tell you that anyone who divorces his wife, except for marital unfaithfulness, and marries another woman commits adultery.'

The only time, it seems, when a Christian can initiate a divorce suit, is in a case of adultery, because whoever commits adultery has broken the marriage bond. The only other time when he or she can be involved in a divorce suit is when an unbelieving partner decides that he or she does not want to continue with the marriage. Paul wrote to the Christians in Corinth at great length on this subject. An extract from his teaching says: '. . . if any brother has a wife who is an unbeliever, and she consents to live with him, he should not divorce her. If any woman has a husband who is an unbeliever, and he consents to live with her, she should not divorce him . . . But if the unbelieving partner desires to separate, let it be so; in such a case the brother or sister is not bound. For God has called us to peace . . .'

It is therefore difficult to see any other grounds for divorce for the Christian who loves the Lord and seeks to live in obedience to him. And the standard is the same for Christians in every culture and every age. We make excuses for divorce because we do not want to admit that we are disobeying the clear instructions of our Lord.

Some Christians, however, decide by God's grace to go the extra mile. Even when a partner has committed adultery, but has fully repented, most mature African Christians agree that there should be no divorce on that ground. If the Lord has forgiven us, we also ought to forgive one another. It is only when someone persists in adultery that divorce should be sought — and that painfully. There have been known cases of Christians (men and women) who at one time or another have caught their partners in this sin. It was very traumatic for them but with time the hurt did heal enough for them to forgive their partners and seek to rebuild the relationship. Through it all, as they turned to the Lord for his help and guidance, they developed new spiritual strength and their relationships matured.

All is not rosy for African Christians, though. There are some who have divorced their partners for various reasons. To call them Christians is perhaps incorrect. In all known cases, pride, greed, selfishness and a serious state of backsliding led them to divorce their partner. Most of them now live miserable lives.

So that is where African Christians stand. In many ways they are already blessed because they have a culture that encourages strong family ties and unity. But their true strength is in the word of God. The more closely Christians follow the Bible's teaching on marriage and family life, the more the Lord grants the blessings of strong families and happy marriages. African Christians believe that strong, well-balanced and love-filled families produce a good society. Society gets bad when families are destroyed. The Devil knows this and therefore attacks families all over the world – Christians and non-Christians alike. Because of this, Christians must see the family as a battlefront and must be prepared to fight anything that will bring disorder or destruction. There will be peace and love in the world only when there is peace and love in the home.

Whether a particular society has rich culture and traditions or not, God's standard and practice can be applied to every culture. Permissiveness and other social ills can be avoided and marriages and families can be strengthened if God is believed and the Bible's teaching taken seriously.

It may seem difficult, but events and experiences have shown that those who put God's standards into everyday practice have found them easy and have found in them the real answer to life's problems.